ISAAC
NEWTON
AND HIS APPLE

by Kjartan Poskitt

Illustrated by Philip Reeve

Hippo

To the nixes at Bootham School 1969–1974, especially Gerard Wakeman (Physics), David Champion and Rodney Wills (Maths), Michael Allen and Peter Heywood (English), and Dr. Chris Moore (alchemy and pyrotechnics for aspiring rock bands). Thanks to you, the loud hairy guitaritst in tatty flared jeans slowly became a bald science biographer in tatty flared jeans.

Scholastic Children's Books,
Euston House, 24 Eversholt Street,
London NW1 1DB, UK

A division of Scholastic Ltd
London ~ New York ~ Toronto ~ Sydney ~ Auckland
Mexico City ~ Hew Delhi ~ Hong Kong

Published by Scholastic Ltd, 1999

Text copyright © Kjartan Poskitt, 1999
Illustrations copyright © Philip Reeve, 1999

10 digit ISBN 0 590 11406 9
13 digit ISBN 978 0590 11406 6

Typeset by M Rules
Printed and bound by CPI Bookmarque Ltd, Croydon, CR0 4TD

24 26 28 30 29 27 25

Papers used by Scholastic Children's Books are made from wood grown in sustainable forests.

CONTENTS

WHY IS ISAAC NEWTON DEAD FAMOUS?

Even though he lived 300 years ago and he wasn't a king or anything obvious like that, nearly everybody has heard of Isaac Newton. What's more, he will always be dead famous until the end of time – but do you know why?

One day Isaac was sitting in his garden under an apple tree when. . .

DONK!

If that happened to you, what would *you* say?

Suppose you were like Isaac and said, 'What made the apple fall?' What would your answer have been?

Once Isaac started to think this apple thing through, there was no stopping him, and of course he eventually came up with the whole notion of gravity.

There – that's why Isaac Newton is dead famous.

So, thanks for reading this book and hopefully it didn't take up too much of your time.

Actually, if you're interested there is a bit more, so if you want to find out. . .

- why he stuck things round the back of his eyeballs and nearly blinded himself

- how he managed to split light up
- how he invented a whole new system of maths
- why he always wanted to keep his brilliant discoveries to himself

- why he wanted to burn his mother
- why the church hated him
- why coin forgers hated him

- in fact, why nearly everybody hated him
- why too many Newtons will kill you
- why he was nearly executed

- whose nose he rubbed against a church wall
- how he got to be so clever in the first place

. . .it's all in here so read on!

A hint before you start

Isaac's life makes a fascinating story and when you've read it you will understand why many people think he was the greatest scientist of all time. Obviously, that means this book is going to have some bits of science in it, not to mention some maths. This gives you two choices:

1 For a nice easy read, don't be scared to skip the technical bits. After all, you can always come back to them later.
2 BUT, if you want to take the full and fabulous Isaac experience to the ultimate extreme – then get stuck in! Quite apart from finding out how clever Isaac was, you might be pleasantly surprised to find how clever you are too!

Are you ready for this?
Good! Get yourself comfy and we're off. . .

THE STRAYNGE TAYLE OF ALICE

Alice made her first entrance into the world when her mother was squashed under a horse's hoof at Grantham market. She was just one of many little brown specks scattered among the dirty cobbles, but Alice didn't mind. It's pretty much what she had expected out of life.

Later in the evening when the market had quietened down, Alice became aware of a large bird tripping its way towards her. (Actually the bird was only a young sparrow, but it was large compared to Alice.) In a second Alice was pecked up from the ground, and moments later she found herself nestled deep inside the warm intestines of the bird. Alice knew she had been lucky. Of her thousands of brothers and sisters, many would be nibbled to lifeless fragments by small rodents, and almost certainly the rest would be left to rot on barren stones, but at least Alice had been given a chance.

Alice was aware of the strong rhythmic motion all around her as the muscles of the bird's body united to power it into flight. Gradually the heaving intestine forced Alice through into a cavity packed with rich, nutritious matter and immediately Alice felt the spark of life at her centre start to ignite.

Suddenly, with one last thrust from the bird's rear muscles, Alice was ejected. Safely encased in a flecked white blob, she fell to the earth below and landed in grass slightly dampened by the night-time dew. Once again Alice had been lucky. Life glowed within her, everything she needed was around her, and she was going to survive.

Of course, Alice was blind, Alice was deaf, Alice had no sense of smell and only the vaguest notion of touch. But Alice did have one thing – Alice had the knowledge she had inherited from her mother. She knew about life, she knew about nature, she knew about why things are and how things come to be. Alice hoped that one day she would be able to bear her own children and pass this same knowledge on to them. Of course, what Alice could never have imagined is that one day she would share a little tiny part of what she knew with someone from a species completely alien to her.

Alice was going to change history, but not before a lot of other things had happened.

A MISERABLE START

CERTIFICATE OF BIRTH

NAME: Isaac Newton

DATE OF BIRTH: 25 December 1642

PLACE OF BIRTH: The Manor House Woolsthorpe, nr Grantham Lincolnshire.

FATHER: Isaac Newton (Died October 1642)

OCCUPATION OF FATHER: Yeoman.

MOTHER: Hannah Newton (or Hannah Ayscough before she was married).

OCCUPATION OF MOTHER Farm manager

DOCTOR'S NOTE: Child not expected to live.

Isaac was born at 20 minutes after midnight on Christmas morning in the year 1642, just a few weeks after his father had died. Isaac's birth had come so prematurely that they could have fitted his tiny body into a 'quart pot', which is about the size of a kettle. Nobody expected the feeble baby to survive until the evening.

However, even at the tender age of just a few hours Isaac astonished people. Not only did he survive until Boxing Day – he went on to live for 84 healthy years.

When Isaac was about one year old, life in England suddenly changed. . .

There was some fighting and house-burning in Lincolnshire, but luckily for the Newtons they missed the worst of the Civil War. Instead Isaac's problems started just after his third birthday when his mother married a 63-year-old vicar called Barnabas Smith. She went off to live in his parish of North Witham – but even though it was only a few miles from Woolsthorpe, little Isaac wasn't invited along. Instead Isaac was left behind with his granny, Mrs Ayscough.

Poor Isaac. Most of the time he spent brooding. . .

MY REAL FATHER'S GONE TO HEAVEN, MY MOTHER DOESN'T WANT ME AND MY GRANNY THINKS I'M STUPID. NO WONDER I'M A MOODY KID WHO STARES INTO SPACE A LOT.

But occasionally he did make his feelings known and he once threatened...

I'LL BURN THE HOUSE DOWN WITH BOTH OF YOU IN IT!

NORTH WITHAM RECTORY

Despite his unhappy situation, Isaac started to show some interests even as a small child, and in particular he was fascinated by sundials. He would sit for hours watching the shadows cast by the sun moving round and would mark their positions at set times of the day. This preoccupation with the movement of the sun was to stay with him his whole life, and even as an old man he would tell the time by looking at shadows rather than a clock.

As it turned out, the Reverend Barnabas died when Isaac was ten, and his mother returned to live at Woolsthorpe. She brought quite a lot of money back with her, and also her new children: Marie aged six, Benjamin aged three, and baby Hannah. For two years they all lived as a family, and in his early teens Isaac was a bit of a father figure to the others, especially little Hannah.

In those days children living in the country were taught the skills they would need to work on farms, and if his father had not died, it's quite possible that Isaac would hardly have learnt to read or write. However, as Isaac's mother had money to spare and didn't know what to do with her moody son, as soon as he was 12 she sent him away to start at the King Edward VI Grammar School in Grantham.

Why was a grammar school called a grammar school? Because that's what you learnt there – grammar. In other words, most of the time you learnt Latin grammar, but for a nice refreshing change they shoved a bit of Greek grammar at you as well.

How about maths, art, woodwork, humanities, science, PE and so on?

Not a chance. Everybody's too busy learning grammar of course!

Actually grammar wasn't quite as useless as it seems. Latin is the language that was used by the ancient Romans, and although nobody was using it for everyday purposes in 1654, it was the one language that all the clever people right across Europe used. This meant that Germans, French, Spanish, Portugese, English and Italians could all understand what each other was up to without everybody having to know everybody else's languages.

This is what Latin looks like:

DIE DULCE FRUERE

And if you think that's bad, this is what ancient Greek looks like:

Ανχιεντ Γρεεκ

It was handy to know a bit of Greek too, because most of the clever stuff that had been thought up before Isaac's time was written down in Greek, even the New Testament of the Bible which would become very important to Isaac. If you could read Greek then you could find out exactly what you wanted to know without somebody else translating it for you (and probably getting it wrong).

It has to be said that at first Isaac wasn't inspired to slog away at learning dead languages, and he soon hit the bottom of the class.

This doesn't mean to say he was lazy – indeed the place he was staying at, Mr Clark's the apothecary, became very full of sundials. (To save you wondering, an apothecary is an old-fashioned chemist.) Actually this is a good time to meet Mr Clark and his family, because most of them come in later on. . .

It was thanks to Mr Clark's stepson Arthur, the school bully, that one day Isaac's whole attitude changed.

Yes, suddenly Isaac had made a decision. He was going to be superior to everybody he knew in any way he could.

Isaac gets some attitude

He didn't just attack Latin – which he learnt to read and write as easily as English – he also amazed everybody with his ability to build model windmills, waterclocks and other mechanical marvels, often working on Sundays rather than studying the Bible as he was expected to. For a laugh, he even made kites with fireworks attached to them and flew them at night, which scared everybody to bits. Another odd thing was that he couldn't resist drawing on walls. His subjects could be inventions, mathematical shapes or even portraits of people, including King Charles I . . . which was a bit dangerous!

By now Oliver Cromwell was running the country. It had taken him six years to defeat King Charles, and he had even gone so far as to have the King executed. (Although the King had his head chopped off, it was sewn on again before they put him in his coffin. That was thoughtful, wasn't it?) Cromwell was a strict

Puritan, which meant that he wanted church services to be as basic and boring as possible so that there was nothing to distract people from worshipping. He especially hated the way his enemies the Roman Catholics had nice robes to wear and went round swinging incense. Even when people were not in church, he had his own ideas on how they should behave. . .

THERE'S TO BE NO DANCING, NO CARNIVALS, AND NO FUN AT CHRISTMAS.

BUT THAT'S HOW IT'S ALWAYS BEEN IN LINCOLNSHIRE...

Needless to say, Oliver Cromwell wouldn't have been too happy at the boy who drew the old king's portrait on walls! However, in many years to come this tiny detail of Isaac's life would prove to be important.

As well as learning Latin and Greek at school, Isaac spent long hours studying chemistry, maths, mechanics and astronomy from a pile of books that had been left at Mr Clark's house by his brainy brother Dr Clark. Isaac described all he found and did with meticulous detail in a little notebook which he bought for tuppence ha'penny, and this little book still survives and is kept in the Pierpont Morgan Library in New York.

At the age of 17 Isaac was amazing everybody when his mother said. . .

FORGET THOSE BOOKS.
I NEED YOU ON
THE FARM!

Needless to say, Isaac was not cut out to be a farmer. He quickly found ways to sneak off and study, but this didn't always go according to plan. He was taken to court because his sheep had escaped and caused damage, his pigs had broken into a neighbour's cornfield and his fences were falling apart. He was fined four shillings and fourpence – which would be about £100 these days. Worse than that, he got a criminal record.

His mother and granny thought he was useless, but Isaac was about to have a bit of luck. His uncle Bill (officially known as the Reverend William Ayscough of Burton Coggles, Lincolnshire) had studied at Trinity College Cambridge and he realized that if Isaac could get there, his brilliance might not be wasted. Along with Isaac's teacher Mr Stokes, he persuaded Isaac's mother to let him return to school to prepare for university.

In 1660 Isaac went to live with Mr Clark the apothecary again. This must have pleased him immensely because not only did Mr Clark have all the books Isaac liked, he also had a young stepdaughter, Catherine Storer, who thought Isaac was gorgeous, and they developed a bit of a romantic attachment. Nothing serious came of it, but it's interesting to mention it because it's about the only time in Isaac's life that he ever did go out with anyone.

The next year Isaac got a place at Trinity College Cambridge. Aged 18, he was about two years older than most of the new students, but more to the point he was a lot poorer. . .

ISAAC'S UNDISCOVERED DIARY

Mother does not send enough money, even though she could easily afford it, so I have to be a 'Sizar' to earn my keep. How can I study when I have to find time to clean rooms and empty chamber-pots for the rich students?

I am in luck though, because I am working for Mrs Clark's brother Humphrey Babington and he is very important in Trinity College. Maybe this will be useful in time.

I write this note as the other students are being fed. Only when they are finished

PTO→

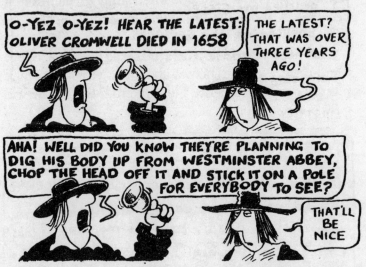

May the sizars clear their plates and see if we have been left anything to eat.

At least some good news, though: H.B is only in college for five weeks this year, so soon I shall have time to myself.

It was an exciting time to be at Cambridge because England had a king again in the form of 'The Merry Monarch', Charles II – son of Charles I. During Cromwell's time most of the teaching jobs at Cambridge had gone to Puritans, but now these were being turfed out and replaced by new people which gave Isaac a chance to progress. Most of the other students spent their lives partying and very few had any intention of getting a degree. Of course, that's why they are all long dead, buried and completely forgotten – but Isaac was different. For nearly four years he studied everything he could lay his hands on, often working right through the night until sunrise – and when he wasn't studying he was desperately trying to sort out his religious beliefs by making long lists of his sins! These included things from years before:

Isaac's list of sins (Volume 1068)

I punched my sister

I shouted at the servants

I broke a candlestick

I refused to take a message for my mother

Finally he graduated in January 1665.

It was at this point that Isaac Newton's brain was race-tuned, supercharged, fuelled up and ready to take on the world.

SO ISAAC, WHAT DO YOU REALLY DO?

Before we find out what Isaac discovered and invented, there's something important to know. Isaac didn't regard himself as a mathematician or a scientist, instead he would say that he was a Natural Philosopher. Like so many of the great brains before him, Isaac was only using maths and science to find out the answers to really big questions such as:

Quite apart from studying maths and so on at Cambridge, Isaac had three other special interests. . .

The Bible

Whether they were Catholic or Protestant, everyone in the country at the time based their beliefs on what they read in the Bible. Isaac was also extremely religious and keen to find out all he could about God, but he did not like being told what to think. He spent ages analysing the Bible and trying to work out religion for himself, and it wasn't long before he decided that even the Bible itself wasn't so perfect after all. This was going to lead to big trouble!

Alchemy

Alchemy was a brilliant subject – it was a sort of cross between chemistry and magic. Alchemists were fascinated as to why some things will not mix (such as water and oil), and why magnets attract. The ancient Greek Aristotle had had a lot to say on the subject and in particular he had the notion that 'everything tends to perfection', which is a wonderfully vague way of explaining anything from things falling down to earth to flowers growing up towards the sun. It was such a cute thought that the idea of being perfect kept coming up in alchemy a lot.

Alchemists often tried experiments that needed some sort of strange force or power from the alchemist himself and for this sort of experiment to work, the alchemist had to be as pure and perfect as possible. This not only meant being extremely religious, but you also had to have the *right* religion. No wonder Isaac studied the

Bible so hard, he wanted to get it right! These experiments could also depend on the positions of stars and planets in the sky, so there's one more thing that would start to link in with Isaac's interests.

Alchemists had two things they were especially keen to discover: one was 'elixir vitae' which was a drink to prolong life, and the other was 'the philosopher's stone' which was a substance so perfect that it had the power to turn boring metals into gold.

Thanks to Aristotle, alchemists believed that everything was made up of a mixture of four basic elements: air, fire, water and earth. For thousands of years they had based their experiments on this, and by Isaac's time only a few of them had begun to think that there might be a different set of chemical elements involved. Aristotle had gone on to say that if you

managed to alter the amounts of the elements in something then you got something else – and that's partly why alchemists hoped that inside every old lump of metal there was a gold bar waiting to get out.

It has to be admitted that sometimes alchemy came up with some useful results and discoveries, but on the whole it was fair old rubbish. Nevertheless, like many clever people before him, Isaac took it all very seriously.

Other philosophers

To help him with his own thoughts, Isaac also studied earlier philosophers, and in Cambridge they were particularly keen on Aristotle. We need to know a bit more about Aristotle and some other blokes, so that's what the next chapter will be about. Before you read it though, be warned – there's a couple of nasty bits in it.

ARISTOTLE AND SOME OTHER BLOKES

Aristotle was a Greek philosopher and scientist who lived from 384 to 322 BC. In his time he studied astronomy, nature, ethics, logic and, as we've already found out, he even had his own ideas about alchemy. One of the main conclusions he came up with was:

The Earth is the centre of the universe and the sun and everything else moves round it.

Aristotle had a very convincing argument for this.

OF COURSE THE EARTH IS STILL! IF IT WERE MOVING AROUND WE WOULD ALL BE THROWN OFF!

Aristarchus

It doesn't matter how clever you are, there will always be some people who don't believe you. A Greek called  Aristarchus lived about 100 years after Aristotle and he was a 'heliocentric' which means he thought the sun was in the middle of the universe and everything else including the Earth went round it, but he found it hard to make anyone take him seriously. ('Helio' comes from the Greek for sun and 'centric' means 'in the middle'.) Quite apart from anything else, the Earth being the centre of everything suited the ancient religious people. These people were very powerful, and so anyone who thought otherwise tended to keep quiet and stay out of trouble.

In Isaac's time, nearly 2,000 years later, Cambridge was still being old-fashioned and sticking to Aristotle's ideas, but elsewhere in Europe they were starting to get more and more suspicious. To find out why, we go back to the time of the ancient Greeks. . .

Ancient people followed the progress of the planets very carefully, which is hardly surprising. If you thought there was a god in a bit of a touchy mood zimming across the sky, you'd keep an eye on him or her too, wouldn't you? (And of course, they didn't have telly in those days, so looking at the sky gave them something to do before bedtime.) They plotted maps which showed the Earth at the centre of the universe, and they drew out the paths of the way the sun and planets seem to move about the sky. The result looked like this:

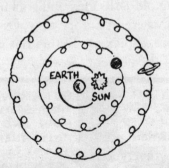

To keep it simple, this picture just shows two planets, Jupiter and Saturn. See how they seem to move in little loops all the time? It looks a bit odd, doesn't it? (Even if it is quite pretty.)

Copernicus

By the 16th century, people were really starting to  wonder why the planets should move in such fancy patterns, and it made much more sense to think of them moving in a simpler fashion. It was about 1510 that the Polish monk Copernicus found out about Aristarchus's heliocentric ideas, and plotted out a version of the planets' movement with the sun in the middle. Although he didn't quite get it right, it did look much more reasonable:

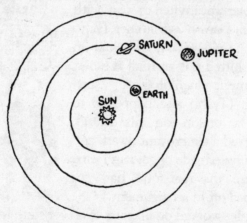

Poor old Copernicus was so worried about his version of space upsetting everybody that he locked it up for 30 years. When the book was eventually published in 1543, it did cause all sorts of trouble, but at least Copernicus kept out of it – he died almost as soon as he saw the first copy of the book.

Johannes Kepler and Tycho Brahe

At the end of the 16th century, about 50 years before

Isaac was born, a copy of Copernicus's book eventually found its way to the German astronomer Johannes Kepler (1571–1630), who was very clever even if he did have a few personal problems. (He had terrible eyesight, worms, spots and piles; his first wife and children died and he spent a lot of his later life trying to stop his mother being burnt as a witch.)

Kepler was invited to work with the rich Danish astronomer Tycho Brahe (1546–1601), who had an island kitted out with all the best equipment available for star-gazing. (Tycho also happened to have a prison on his island, employed a clairvoyant dwarf, and had a nose made of gold and wax, because his real one had got chopped off in an argument.)

Kepler worked on all sorts of clever stuff, for instance:

- he discovered how eyes work – and why you need two of them to judge distances
- he showed how good telescopes and spectacles could be made
- he devised ways of calculating the distance of stars

However, from Isaac's point of view, the main thing Kepler did was come up with his three laws of planetary motion and we'll find out about these later on.

Galileo

There are two other blokes we have to know about before we get back to Isaac. One is the Italian Galileo

THHHRRRRRRRP!

Galilei (1564–1642), who is generally known as Galileo for short. So what do we know about him?

He was rude, arrogant, loud-mouthed, tactless, obstinate, argumentative, and he nicked other people's ideas, but most of all he was infuriatingly clever. A whole book about Galileo would be brilliant, but if you remember, this book is supposed to be about Isaac Newton so we'll just note two things that Galileo did:

- Galileo showed that the acceleration of falling objects is constant by dropping things out of high buildings (we'll see what this means later on too).
- Galileo told everybody that Aristotle's idea of the Earth being still was wrong. (He was right about that, but he fell out with the Pope and was eventually bullied into changing his mind.) He said that you can tell the Earth is moving because that's what makes the tides of the sea go up and down. (Actually he was wrong about that, and the Pope was very pleased to tell him so.)

If you want to get a tiny idea of what Galileo really looked like, one of his fingers is on display in a museum in Florence. Isn't that nice?

Descartes

The last bloke we need to know about is René Descartes. He lived from 1596 to 1650 and he really

attacked Aristotle where it hurt. Most of Aristotle's stuff had been based on some wonderfully airy-fairy ideas such as everything coming from earth, fire, water and air, and everything 'tending to perfection' and 'seeking its rightful place'.

Descartes was a lot more up to date and said nature was like a machine. Everything could be measured, and there was a nice solid mechanical reason for everything that happened. As it turns out, he pretty much got it right, so 'hurrah' for Descartes.

(Descartes then went on to try and work out some nice solid mechanical reasons for the movement of planets and so on, and sadly for him he got them all completely wrong, so 'ya-boo' to Descartes.)

Needless to say, Descartes upset all sorts of people who couldn't see how God fitted into his scheme of things, and these included a clever Cambridge bunch called the "Platonists". Isaac had a lot of time for the Platonists, who included Isaac Barrow (who you'll meet later) and Henry More (who you won't meet later even though he was a lovely bloke apparently). Like the others, Isaac wasn't happy with the God situation, but he did realize that Descartes's basic ideas were a lot better than Aristotle's. In many ways, it was Descartes who made Isaac incorporate maths into his philosophical studies.

Right, that's enough about Aristotle and the other blokes for now, so we'll go and catch up with Isaac again.

ISAAC'S FRIEND

A nice cosy little chapter with no complicated stuff in it.

Apart from learning about Aristotle and the other blokes, the other thing that happened to Isaac Newton at Cambridge was that he got a good friend.

John Wickins had come from Manchester to be a student around the same time as Isaac. When John had first got to Cambridge he found he was sharing rooms with a stupid loud-mouth whom he hated, and so he used to go off on walks to avoid him. One day he came across Isaac who was equally fed up for the same reason, and so they decided to take rooms together.

Wickins himself was studying religion intensely, but he would always be surrounded by Isaac's books and bottles and other equipment. Luckily for Isaac, Wickins was a big lad, and used to help set everything up and even monitor experiments and make clear copies of Isaac's notes. Wickins also tried his best to ensure Isaac ate properly and got some sleep, but usually failed.

One really odd thing that Wickins put up with occurred when Isaac had their rooms redecorated. It turned out that Isaac was completely obsessed with one colour – crimson! The chairs, the beds, the cushions, the curtains and everything else were all bright red. Isaac even had recipes for making red paint involving sheep's blood, which must have been a bit unnerving.

TIME FOR A SPOT OF DECORATING!

Although they shared together for 20 years, Wickins never said much about his time with Isaac – even in later life when his son asked him about it. This is strange because he must have had a great deal to say!

Sadly, they did eventually fall out, but we haven't got that far yet.

A FLYING START

When Isaac first graduated from Cambridge in January 1665, he didn't mess about.

So what are all these things he developed in his first months out of university? Let's look at them one at a time, and because most of us aren't as clever as Isaac, we'll keep it as simple as possible.

Before the binomial theorem

In the years leading up to Isaac's time some handy methods of calculation had been invented which were to be very useful, especially with the murderous maths involved in astronomy. Before we meet Isaac's Big Bright and Beautiful Binomial Breakthrough, you might want to see some of the other things that had recently been discovered. (If you think they look too scary, then shut your eyes and hurry to page 46.)

41

Decimals

In 1585 a Flemish man called Stevin suggested the idea of using decimal fractions.

$$\frac{1}{2} = 0.5 \qquad\qquad \frac{1}{11} = 0.090909$$

$$\frac{1}{3} = 0.333333$$

$$\frac{1}{12} = 0.083333$$

$$\frac{1}{10} = 0.1$$

Of course, we're all familiar with decimals now because that's what you get on calculators. For instance if you put in 1 ÷ 5 you get 0.2 which is a decimal way of writing one-fifth.

Logarithms

Another brilliant invention came from a Scottish baron called Napier who invented logarithms. These are a

short cut to multiplying and dividing complicated numbers. Logarithms also made it much easier to work out 'powers' which are always jamming up astronomical calculations. Nasty looking things like x^3 or even $\sqrt{y}$ were almost impossible to deal with before 'logs', and it was such a good system that people only stopped using it about 25 years ago when calculators became common.

BARON NAPIER AND HIS
LOG O' RHYTHMS

That bloke Descartes again

As well as rubbishing Aristotle, the philosopher Descartes had invented the 'cartesian co-ordinate' system which is a way of measuring where things are, and this led to being able to draw algebra equations out as graphs. Have you noticed? Descartes invented the cartesian system? They loved to get their names used, didn't they? Anyway, here's how this equation/graph thing works:

The first thing you need to do is draw two axes on your graph paper.

No, no, NO! Not those sort of axes. First you draw a line going straight up, and that's called an axis. You then draw a line going along, and that's another axis. When you have two of them they are called axes and when you say it, it sounds like axeeees.

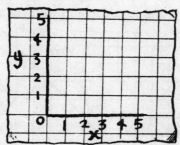

The line going up is the 'y' axis, and the line going along is the 'x' axis. They both have numbers along them starting with zero where they meet.

If you're going to be using negative numbers too, then you make your axes a bit longer like this.

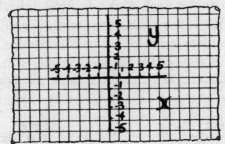

Once you've done that, you can then draw your equation out. Let's start with a really simple equation: $y = x$. First you pick a number for x, let's say $x = 1$ to start with. You then work out what y should be. Obviously if your equation is $y = x$ then y will be 1 too! You then mark a dot on the graph above the 1 on the x axis and along from the 1 on the y axis.

Pick another number for x, say 2, and work out y which in this case is also 2. Put a dot in the right place. Do some more dots for other values of x and y if you like.

When you've done enough dots, you'll see a pattern emerge, and if you join them up you get a line.

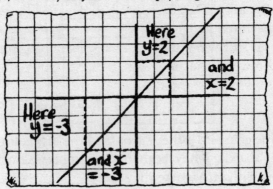

Because $y = x$ is such a simple equation, you get a nice simple straight line.

How about curved lines? Let's try this equation: $y = x^2$. (This is the same as $y = x$ times x. The little 2 means you have to multiply two x's together. If it was a little 3, then it would be 'x times x times x' and so on.)

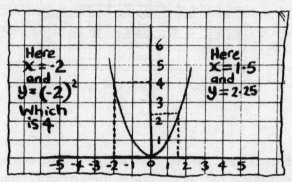

Here you can see the line joins up all the points on the graph where the value of y equals the value of x^2. For instance, where $x = 1$, then $y = 1^2$ which is 1. Where $x = 2$, $y = 2^2$ which is 4. The line also shows all the values in between, so for instance where $x = 1.5$ then $y = 1.5^2$ which is 2.25.

This particular curve is called a parabola, and you may be interested to know that if you turn it upside down, it shows the exact path of how a ball flies when it is thrown in the air.

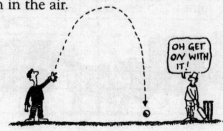

So what's the use of all this?

Well it's got lots of different uses actually, but most importantly for Isaac, **maths equations can be used to describe how things move.**

And now – Isaac's binomial theorem

So much for what other people had invented. By now you'll be gagging to see Isaac's binomial theorem, so here's how it starts:

$$(a + b)^n = a^n + \frac{na^{n-1}b}{1} + \frac{n(n-1)a^{n-2}b^2}{1 \times 2} + \frac{n(n-1)(n-2)a^{n-3}b^3}{1 \times 2 \times 3} + \frac{n(n-1)(n-2)(n-3)a^{n-4}b^4}{1 \times 2 \times 3 \times 4} + \ldots$$

And so it goes on for ever with each extra number getting more and more complicated to work out, and when you do work them out you'll find the value you get for each one gets smaller and smaller and smaller and smaller and. . .

Good, isn't it?

Now obviously you'd love to know exactly what this theorem is about and precisely how it works, but sadly we haven't got space here so all we'll say is that with the binomial theorem you could calculate logarithms really exactly and so work out extremely complicated sums. Isaac himself got a bit carried away with it, and worked out some sums to 55 decimal places.

Tangents

In May 1665 Isaac came to terms with tangents.

A tangent is a straight line that touches a curve at one point. Here are some:

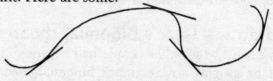

So what have tangents got to do with anything?

Everybody was studying the moon and planets and their paths and were desperate to work out why they moved as they did. Old Aristotle saying 'everything seeks its rightful place' didn't do for them any more.

Astronomers spent ages drawing the curved paths of the planets out on paper and then wrestling away with fiendish sums to describe what they saw. They hoped that if they could describe exactly how planets moved with maths equations, then it might help to understand what was making them move in the first place – YAHOO!

Isaac realized that if you look at a planet for a split second, it is moving at a tangent to the curve. Sounds nasty, eh? Well think of it like this. . .

Let's say that instead of gradually turning a corner, the planet moved round in a set of straight lines like this:

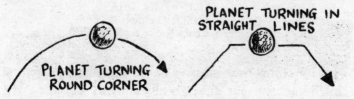

PLANET TURNING IN STRAIGHT LINES

PLANET TURNING ROUND CORNER

Obviously as the planet moves along each line, its direction is straight ahead, which makes the sums a lot easier. To make the path of the planet look more like a curve, you can use much shorter lines.

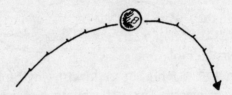

You can make the lines shorter and shorter, and as you do the path will become a perfect curve – but the point is that even if your lines are only teeny-weeny, they are still straight.

If you want to see exactly which direction the planet is travelling at any one instant, all you do is extend the teeny-weeny straight line it's sitting on and ABRACADABRA . . . you get a tangent!

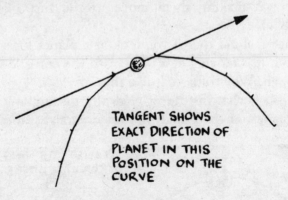

TANGENT SHOWS EXACT DIRECTION OF PLANET IN THIS POSITION ON THE CURVE

This led to his next massive discovery, which Isaac first called *fluxions* but the world came to know as the dreaded. . .

Calculus

Here are some important things to know about CALCULUS:

- Grown men and women who pretend they were dead clever at school secretly fear it.
- Students tremble and quake at the sheer mention of its name.
- Many nice sane people have been turned into gibbering wrecks trying to come to grips with it.
- Spelt backwards it reads SULUCLAC, and if you say suluclac 20 times very quickly you'll get a knot in your tongue.
- When maths teachers realize it's the week to start explaining calculus, most of them try and go off sick, or offer to teach French or take gym class instead or even say they have to go to a funeral.
- It isn't really all that bad. Honest.

OK, it's a bit mean shoving calculus at you when you've just clapped eyes on the binomial theorem. Luckily history gives us a convenient break here to find out something else that affected Isaac first.

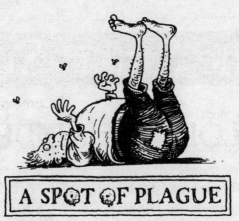

A SPOT OF PLAGUE

A merry little chapter to take your mind off calculus.

With all this chat about how clever people were and how they were making fantastic calculations about the movement of planets and so on, it is easy to forget that life in the slums of London was absolutely disgusting. The streets would stink of sewage and animal mess; in a hot summer the flies and insects would gather in thick buzzing clouds and all sorts of skin diseases were rife. Most importantly, there would be rats crawling all over the place.

London docks were very busy in those days, and even if anybody had noticed a couple of brown rats sneaking ashore from a boat, nobody could have imagined that the fleas on their backs would be responsible for the hideous deaths of over 80,000 people in London alone.

The Stuart Sun

December 1664

SAILORS FOUND DEAD

Two French sailors were found dead in the gutter near Drury Lane Theatre yesterday. 'They looked right 'orrible with big bleedin' lumps round their necks, they did,' said Mrs Annie Clackett who found them.

Mrs Clackett, 37, has since been feeling ill herself. 'I hope I haven't caught something off those Frenchies,' she said.

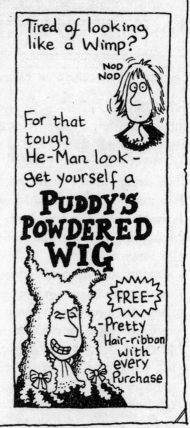

Tired of looking like a Wimp?

NOD NOD

For that tough He-Man look – get yourself a

PUDDY'S POWDERED WIG

FREE –

– Pretty Hair-ribbon with every Purchase

The first two victims were found in December 1664, and it didn't take long before others joined them.

The Stuart Sun

December 1664 : Late edition

MYSTERY ILLNESS STRIKES!

but rumours of plague are yet to be confirmed.

'The public are advised not to panic,' said a government official who examined her. 'I'm sure it's harmless.'

A woman was found collapsed in the street yesterday, shivering, sweating and covered in her own vomit. She is believed to be Mrs Annie Clackett who discovered the dead French sailors last week. An enquiry has been opened into the cause of her condition,

EAT PUDDY'S PORK PIES

They contain hardly any Worms or Grubs— Guaranteed!

Meanwhile in the squalor of the London drains the culprits were multiplying fast. The fleas from the continent had brought with them the bubonic plague, and by hitching rides on the backs of the town rat population they quickly spread right through the capital. Just one tiny flea bite was all it took. . .

52

The Stuart Sun

January 1665

GOVERNMENT OFFICAL DEAD

The official who examined Annie Clackett less than a week ago has been found dead having suffered the same symptoms.

Further victims have fallen in Lambeth, Southwark, Westminster and many other parts of the town. Another government official has said,

'It turns out that it is the plague. We are now advising the public to panic.'

PLAGUE VICTIM? TRY PUDDY'S PAINT

IDEAL FOR MARKING CROSSES ON YOUR DOOR

BUY SOME NOW IF IT'S THE LAST THING YOU DO!

Yes, the Great Plague of 1665 was under way and although no one really knew how it was transmitted, if they had known they would have been unable to do much about it.

Bubonic facts:

- Bubonic plague gets it name from 'buboes' which are nasty lumps that grow around the groin, armpit or neck.
- Symptoms include high temperature, shivering, headaches, everything-else-aches and vomiting.
- Lucky victims have a 25% chance of getting better after about a week.
- Unlucky victims have a 75% chance of death.
- The best cure? Don't catch it in the first place. If you do, you might like to try 'Lacatellus Balsam' which Isaac swore by all his life ever since he learnt to make it in Mr Clark's shop. It includes turpentine, beeswax, olive oil and red wine. You can either drink it, or it's also handy to rub on mad-dog bites. Yum!

The Stuart Sun

June 1665

PLAGUE SPREADS

Thousands of Londoners are already dead, and now victims are starting to die in the provinces. Many towns are being evacuated and establishments are closing, including the university at Cambridge.

IT'S SAFER IN SCOTLAND!

SOME SPACES STILL AVAILABLE IN **PUDDY'S** WAGON HEADING NORTH TOMORROW! (THOSE WITH LUMPY NECKS NEED NOT APPLY)

And so it was that Isaac left Cambridge to return to the family home at Lincolnshire. You might think that having to leave the university was a good excuse for messing about and having a holiday, but that's not what Isaac was like. Even while he was at Cambridge, most of what he learnt he taught himself from books, and he was always best working alone. Going home meant that he could really shut himself away and get on with some serious stuff, and as it turned out, Isaac had the most brilliantly productive 16 months ever achieved by anyone.

Just before we move on, let's give one last thought to the Great Plague. Imagine what it must have been like walking through the backstreets of London in 1665. It can't have been pleasant. As well as the usual smells and filth there would be screams of people dying, crying from the relatives, the stink of abandoned corpses – and although you wouldn't know it, if you felt that sudden little itch of a flea bite, you'd be next.

There! After that, a bit of calculus doesn't seem so bad, does it?

By the time you've got to page 63, you'll have got through the hardest bit of the book. Remember, we are trying to understand the workings of a genius here, so don't worry too much if you don't quite follow it all!

Here we go then, and good luck. . .

CALCULUS: THE MATHS MIRACLE

Calculus is a form of maths that starts off with a really simple idea – then gets extremely ugly in the middle and comes out with a reasonably simple end. When Isaac was inventing it, he had to put on his mental wellies and wade through the ugly bit, but you'll be glad to know that we can just skip to the simple ending. Once calculus was discovered it became a massive weapon in the fight against gruesome calculations and to a mathematician, calculus is more useful than a steering wheel to a bus driver.

The whole point of calculus is that you find out answers by splitting things up into smaller and smaller bits until you get a result. In their way the ancient Greeks had a go at it, especially when studying circles.

A slice of pi

Antiphon lived in Greece around 400 BC and he tried to find the area of a circle by filling it up with triangles because it was easy to find the area of triangles and add them up. First he put in a big triangle. . .

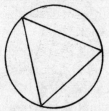

Then he filled up the gaps with smaller triangles, and then even smaller triangles and then *even smaller* smaller triangles. . .

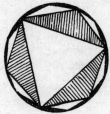

But it didn't matter how long he kept on going, he was never ever going to quite fill the circle, and so work out the exact area!

At about the same time as Antiphon, another Greek called Bryson hit on the idea of enclosing a circle with two multi-sided shapes, because he knew that the area of the circle had to be slightly more than the inner shape and less than the outer shape.

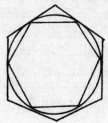

Again he had the same problem. He tried it with 12-sided shapes and then 24-sided shapes . . . and the more sides his shapes had, the closer he got to an answer; but he could never be exact.

Nearly 200 years after that came the turn of the great Archimedes, who lived between 287 and 212 BC. Instead of the area he decided to concentrate on working out the circumference of a circle.

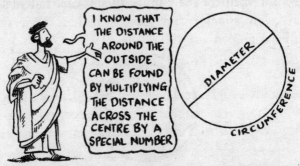

I KNOW THAT THE DISTANCE AROUND THE OUTSIDE CAN BE FOUND BY MULTIPLYING THE DISTANCE ACROSS THE CENTRE BY A SPECIAL NUMBER

This special number was given the Greek name 'pi' which is written π and is pronounced 'pie', but the problem was working out its exact value. Archimedes tried it using a method like Bryson's but as he was better at sums he ended up using shapes with 96 sides. Archimedes did come very close to an answer (he worked out that π was somewhere between $3^{10}/_{71}$ and $3\frac{1}{7}$) but even he could never quite get an exact measurement.

People kept trying to improve on Archimedes's method and not long before Isaac lived, the German Ludolf Van Ceulen spent 20 years calculating π using shapes with over 32 BILLION sides.

Obviously this was all getting very silly, so thank goodness Isaac came along with his new method.

Calculus is a mathematical way of doing exactly the

same thing as all these earlier people were doing – i.e. using smaller and smaller and smaller measurements to get closer to the answer. The trouble is that you need *infinitely* small measurements to get an exact answer – and Isaac worked out how to do it.

Even though Isaac could have used calculus to work out π, he wasn't too bothered because just before he was born people had found other ways to do it. Isaac had had a go too, and here's one of his nice simple calculations:

$$\frac{\pi}{6} = \frac{1}{2} + \frac{1}{2}\left(\frac{1}{3 \times 2^3}\right) + \frac{1 \times 3}{2 \times 4}\left(\frac{1}{5 \times 2^5}\right) + \frac{1 \times 3 \times 5}{2 \times 4 \times 6}\left(\frac{1}{7 \times 2^7}\right) + \ldots$$

The real reason Isaac developed his calculus was to find exactly how the tangents change direction as you go along a curve, which is the problem that we saw on page 48.

Right then, the first thing we need is a curve, so here's the nice simple parabola we saw before:

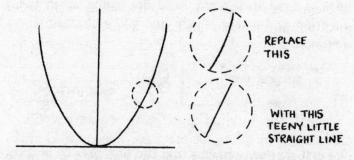

REPLACE THIS

WITH THIS TEENY LITTLE STRAIGHT LINE

Let's have a look at a teeny little bit of it. First we'll replace the bit of curve with a straight line. What Isaac was trying to investigate was how steep the line was – in other words what was the gradient of this little line?

Gradients

Suppose you're walking up a steep hill, this is how you measure the gradient.

5m

GRADIENT = $\frac{1}{2}$

10 m

You divide how high you've risen by how far you have walked along. In this case you divide the 5 m you've gone up by the 10 m you've gone along. You get $5 \div 10$ which gives a gradient of $\frac{1}{2}$.

(Sometimes you see road signs with gradients marked, and usually these fractions are given in percentages. If you see a gradient of 20% this means that your gradient is $\frac{1}{5}$, which means that for every 5 m you go along, you'll go up 1 m.)

To measure the gradient of one of Isaac's teeny little lines, we put in a teeny little line going up in the y direction and a teeny little line going along in the x direction.

OUR TEENY LITTLE STRAIGHT LINE →

δy

δx

GRADIENT = $\dfrac{\delta y}{\delta x}$

We call the teeny height that the line rises δy and the teeny distance along δx. (The funny sign δ is the Greek letter 'delta', and in maths it means 'a teeny little bit of'.)

So, in the same way as if you were walking up a hill,

the gradient of a teeny line on the curve is calculated as $\delta y / \delta x$.

Isaac took this one step further. He imagined his teeny lines getting smaller and smaller until they were just infinitely small points that couldn't get any smaller. The gradient of these teeniest possible lines is called dy/dx. Can you see the difference? Look carefully at the letter 'd's. It's only a tiny difference, but there again we are talking about tiny things, so it does make sense in a strange way.

Now here's the *really* clever bit.

With the curves that Isaac was working on, obviously the gradient alters as you move along.

THAT'S TRUE- IT IS GETTING STEEPER!

What Isaac wanted to figure out was how to make equations that described the rate of change of the gradient.

TONS AND TONS OF REALLY MIND-BENDING MATHS LATER. . .

. . .he cracked it.

Suppose you have a curve described by the equation $y = x^6$.

To get the gradient at any point on the line you need to work out the value of dy/dx. This process has the ridiculous name of DIFFERENTIATION, which is quite enough to put anybody off but it's dead simple. All you need to do are two little jobs:

- Copy the little '6' down to the front.
- Subtract one from the little 6 left on the top.

In this case our finished answer is $\frac{dy}{dx} = 6x^5$.

In just the same way, if our curve was $y = x^4$ we would get $\frac{dy}{dx} = 4x^3$. That's all there is to it, so there you are! You've just learnt how to do DIFFERENTIAL CALCULUS. Aren't you brilliant?

Let's remember why Isaac invented all this: if he could work out $\frac{dy}{dx}$ then he could measure gradients at any point on a curve, and more importantly he could analyse how the gradient was changing as the curve went along. This gave calculus another slightly different use. You can plot graphs which show how fast things are moving by putting distance along one axis and time along the other. This graph shows a car speeding up.

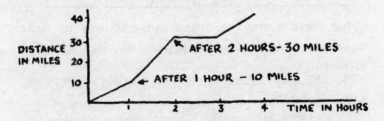

You'll see that in the first hour the car has only gone 10 miles. However in the second hour, the car has gone another 20 miles – so obviously it is going faster. The increase in speed (which is called acceleration) is shown by the line getting steeper, and Isaac found he could link all these things up using differentiation. BINGO! Isaac had hit a mathematical jackpot.

Isaac would soon find that solving problems of acceleration would help him understand why planets moved like they did, and in turn this would help him to discover THE BIG 'G'.

Isaac's miracle of maths was going to be very handy indeed.

Secrecy!

There's something slightly strange you should know about Isaac, and now's probably the best time to find out.

As we saw when he was attacked by Arthur at school, Isaac had a really foul temper, and could lose it very easily. No wonder he liked to work alone and he only had one close friend! So what do you think he did when he'd developed the most fabulous and groovy mathematical gimmick of the age? Did he jump up and down and tell everybody? Did he try and sell it? Did he have it tattooed on his bottom?

No.

(Well, of course we can't be absolutely sure about the tattoo . . .)

Like nearly everything else that he found or invented, he wrote it out in a private notebook and didn't tell anybody.

This might seem strange, but you probably know what it's like when you do something you're really pleased with – there's always a few creeps who slither up to you and say 'it isn't that good' or 'you missed a bit' or even 'who cares?' They love to say you're wrong even when you're not and generally you have to spend too much time sticking up for yourself and not getting on with anything else.

Isaac and his temper couldn't cope with even the merest hint of criticism, and so that's why he didn't tell anybody what he was up to. Besides, he hated the idea of being famous or well known, he just wanted to be left alone to get on with his work. Unfortunately, this still managed to lead to a lot of shouting, screaming and general aggravation.

The Lucasian Professor

Actually, it isn't quite true to say Isaac didn't tell anybody about his work. At Cambridge there was one person he trusted, and that was his old tutor Isaac Barrow, who was the first 'Lucasian Professor of Mathematics'.

- The job of 'Lucasian Professor' got its name from Henry Lucas who had been the MP for Cambridge University, and who had left a lot of money to pay the wages for whoever took it.
- Ever since it was created in 1663, it has always been one of the most respected jobs in the world.
- It's been almost 350 years since it started, and yet there have only been 17 Lucasian Professors: they've all been brilliant in one way or another.
- The current Lucasian Professor is Stephen Hawking, the wheelchair-bound genius who is solving the fiendish puzzles that explain how the universe started and who is already a mathematical legend.

When our Isaac first started his studies at Cambridge, Barrow thought he was a bit useless and neglected the books he should have been reading. However, after a couple of years it dawned on Barrow that Isaac was already too clever for them, and rather than being a complete waster, like most of the students at the time, Isaac was an academic diamond.

Barrow was rather jolly and as well as being brainy he got up to all sorts of outrageous stunts; one time he even won a fist-fight in Turkey. Despite their different natures, Isaac got on with him not only because Barrow was good at maths, but because he also had interests in alchemy and religion, worked ridiculously long hours, gave Isaac birthday presents and most importantly, he was ambitious. Barrow was always looking for the next job up the ladder and young Isaac knew it would make sense to stick with him. Isaac even helped Barrow develop some optical research that he knew was all wrong because he didn't want to risk losing this important contact.

Isaac and Barrow also had one other thing in common:

I SAY, WHO ARE THOSE SCWUFFY OIKS?

WHY, 'TIS NEWTON AND THE LUCASIAN MATHS PROFESSOR, THE SCWUFFIEST DWESSERS IN CAMBWIDGE!

The stolen method

Isaac had shown Barrow some of his work on calculus (or 'fluxions' as he called it) and some years later Barrow passed them on to the maths publisher John Collins. Collins wanted to publish it all so the whole world could see it, but Isaac absolutely refused which was to lead to a very bitter dispute.

The Stuart Sun

October 1684

GERMAN DISCOVERS MIRACLE MATHS

Gottfried Leibniz has invented an ingenious maths system with which he claims he can analyse motion and speed. 'I call it calculus,' he said yesterday, and added, 'I thought it up all by myself. I am indeed a genius.'

Yes, it seemed that the German had indeed discovered calculus independently, but unlike the secretive Isaac, Leibniz had his version published in 1684 which is why the name 'calculus' stuck. What upset Isaac even more was that Leibniz took all the credit for the method. Isaac didn't allow his own version to come out until 1704, and that's when the dirty fighting really started.

HERR LEIBNIZ SAYS YOUR MR NEWTON STOLE HIS IDEAS!

THEN LEIBNIZ IS A LIAR, ISN'T HE?

This sort of exchange went on until Leibniz died 12 years later, but shortly after that Isaac found out what he had suspected all along: Collins had sneakily showed Leibniz some of Isaac's fluxions work years before! As you can imagine, Isaac wasn't best pleased and English mathematicians were still squabbling with the rest of Europe about it for hundreds of years, even though there's no real reason to think Leibniz really did steal what he had seen.

The one good thing that Leibniz did do was to introduce the dy/dx and $\delta y/\delta x$ way of explaining calculus, which we've already seen in this book. Isaac's method of writing it down was much more confusing! Anyway, all these details of cheating and accusations over calculus have got us a bit ahead of ourselves, so we'll flip back to autumn 1665.

Isaac is still at home avoiding the plague, and equally importantly, avoiding anyone who might disturb his work. Evenings are just starting to get longer, the crops in the fields are ready for harvest, and high up in a certain tree an apple is preparing to break the frontiers of scientific knowledge. . .

THE BIG 'G'

The story of the big 'G' actually runs over several years, and trying to pin down exactly when Isaac developed each new idea isn't easy because he was so secretive about it. What we can be fairly sure of is that it started back in the autumn of 1665, when Isaac was sitting in the garden at Woolsthorpe.

By this time he had pretty much read everything worth reading about anything, and made some firm decisions as to what he agreed with and what he didn't.

However, there had been two people whose work he did appreciate and pondered on for days on end.

Remember Johannes Kepler? After 20 hard years of sky-watching and sums, in 1609 he published his laws about how the planets move. Of course, as Isaac was dead clever, he understood these laws immediately, but we might need to take them a bit gently, so first of all we'll start with some very simple versions:

Kepler's laws – the simple versions

1 As a planet orbits around the sun, it moves in closer then moves back out again. (Some of them hardly move in at all, and others move in quite a lot, but don't worry about that.)

2 When a planet is nearer the sun it moves a bit faster.

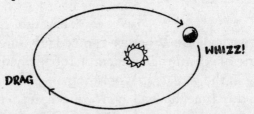

3 The planets that are further away from the sun take longer to complete orbits than those that are closer in. Not only do they have further to go, they move slower.

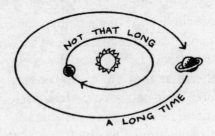

There, how was that? Now, if you're in the mood let's look at Kepler's laws properly and see more precisely what they said. (Of course, if you're not in the mood you can always come back to these pages later when you're old and fuddy and have nothing better to do.)

Kepler's laws – the way he told them
1: Planets travel in ellipses round the sun.

Instead of just going round the sun in a perfect circle, Kepler realized each planet moved in an ellipse – which is a bit like a squashed circle which has two centres.

Here's how to draw an ellipse:

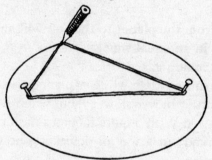

You stick two pins in the paper and put a loose loop of string round them. Put your pencil in the loop and, keeping the string tight, draw round the two pins. The shape you get is an ellipse.

The place where you put each pin is called a 'focus' of the ellipse, and if you want to be posh you'll say that an ellipse has two 'foci'. By the way, if you put your pins so close together that they are on top of each other, then instead of an ellipse you get a perfect circle.

Kepler's first law went on to say that. . .

The sun is positioned at one focus of the ellipse.

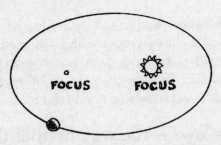

As you can see, this means that sometimes a planet is nearer the sun than at others. By the way, we've exaggerated the ellipses in these pictures, because most of the planets' paths are *nearly* circles, but that would look boring to draw.

2: A line from the planet to the sun will sweep out an equal area in an equal time.
This law is amazing.

Kepler realized that while a planet is further away from the sun, it moves slower – but when it is closer in it moves faster. With a quite fabulous flash of brilliance Kepler worked out a way of describing how much the speed changed.

Suppose the sun and a planet were stuck on a piece of paper, and a bit of very inky elastic string was fixed between them. What would happen after one month, for example?

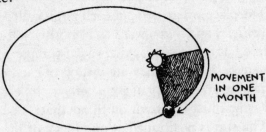

MOVEMENT IN ONE MONTH

72

You would get an area on the paper covered in ink.

Now then, suppose you let the planet continue round the sun a bit, then fixed up the inky elastic again. If you then waited another month, you would get a second inky area.

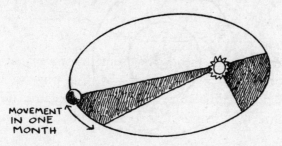

MOVEMENT
IN ONE
MONTH

Kepler is saying that as both these areas took one month to cover, then they will be the same size. Of course, one is longer and thinner because *the planet is further away from the sun and going slower.* The other is shorter and fatter because *the planet is nearer the sun and going faster.*

This isn't just a rough guide to planet speed either, it is an absolutely accurate measure, although how Kepler thought of it is anybody's guess.

3: $\dfrac{T^2}{r^3} = k$

Nice and simple, isn't it? If you prefer it in words:

The square of the time taken for a planet to complete one orbit of the sun is proportional to the cube of its average distance from the sun.

You've got to admit, it's catchy.

There's no escaping the fact that you need to know a bit of maths to understand this one, but if you've got this far then you'll eat it up for breakfast.

The best way to understand Kepler's third law is to have two pretend planets going round a pretend sun.

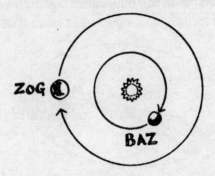

Here's what a sum based on the law might look like:

$$\frac{(\text{Time for Baz to orbit the sun})^2}{(\text{Distance from Baz to sun})^3} = \frac{(\text{Time for Zog to orbit the sun})^2}{(\text{Distance from Zog to sun})^3}$$

You see that for Baz, the time for the orbit is squared and put over the average distance cubed, and that comes to the same as if you did it for Zog. If our pretend sun had more planets, you could put all of them in the equation too and it would look even uglier than it does now. Yuk! Anyway, let's put some numbers in and see if it gets any prettier.

Let's say that:

Baz is 1 billion km from the sun and Zog is 2 billion km from the sun.

We'll also say that Baz takes 10 years to orbit the sun.

Thanks to Kepler, we can work out how long Zog takes. All we do is fill the numbers we know into that horrible looking thing above. We'll put the time in years and the distances in billions of miles and so we get:

$$\frac{10^2}{1^3} = \frac{(\textit{Time for Zog to orbit the sun})^2}{2^3}$$

Which comes down to. . .
(Time for Zog to orbit the sun)^2 = 800.
So the time for Zog's orbit is $\sqrt{800}$ (which is the same as saying we need to know what number times by itself makes 800) which comes to 28.28 years.

So much for Kepler's third law then, and you'll be relieved to know there aren't any more Kepler laws to trouble us. In fact, it's time for us to say goodbye to poor old Kepler altogether, because his life gradually fizzled out to a pretty miserable end. He spent his last weeks painfully dragging himself from town to town trying to collect wages he was owed until he eventually collapsed and died. At least his brilliance provided some of Isaac's main inspiration, and for that he'll always be remembered.

Galileo

The other person whose work Isaac latched on to was Galileo, who coincidentally had died in the year of Isaac's birth. That makes you think, doesn't it? Maybe when Galileo died, a bit of his spirit drifted around the world and finally landed in the newborn Isaac? It could explain where Isaac not only got his brilliance, but also his terrible temper! Anyway, back to the facts.

Apart from being one of the first people to dare suggest that the Earth moved round the sun, Galileo's great discovery was that a falling body accelerates at a uniform rate.

'Oh no!' you're thinking. 'Don't say there's going to be more maths equations!'

Relax. Happily Mr Reeve can explain how Galileo's idea developed with some of his nice pictures. . .

That was the basis of Galileo's discovery, and people like to think he performed this sort of experiment at the Leaning Tower of Pisa. Maybe he did, maybe he didn't, but it's a nice thought.

Having realized that different objects would fall the same distance at the same time, Galileo went a step further and realized that when you drop something, it speeds up steadily as it falls.

77

To prove it, here's an experiment you might like to try yourself, although younger readers might need an adult to help. You need:

- an elephant fitted with a speedometer
- an aeroplane with a big door
- a stopwatch
- binoculars
- a very big mop and bucket

All you do is put your elephant in the aeroplane and take off. When you are a few thousand metres in the air, shove your elephant out of the door. Start your stopwatch and keep an eye on the elephant's speedometer with your binoculars.

Here's what you will find:

- after one second the elephant will be falling at 10 metres per second. . .
- after two seconds the elephant will be falling at 20 metres per second. . .
- after three seconds the elephant will be falling at 30 metres per second. . .
- after four seconds the elephant will be falling at 40 metres per second. . .
. . .and so on.

You will find the elephant's speed increases by 10 metres per second for every second it is falling. It doesn't matter if the elephant has just started to fall, or is already plummeting at a terrifying rate – the speed will always be increasing by 10 metres per second every second. This is called constant acceleration.

(Actually we have simplified things a bit here. It isn't quite 10 metres per second per second, the exact figure involved is 9.80665 but that's a bit tedious to keep tripping over when you're reading a jolly book like this.)

There are two things that will affect this constant acceleration. One is if the elephant is going really fast, then air resistance will start to slow it down a bit (especially if it sticks its ears out), but your aeroplane would need to be very high up indeed for this to happen. The other thing that will affect the constant acceleration is the ground. When the elephant hits it . . . well that's why you need a very big mop and bucket.

Time to check up on Isaac

So there's our Isaac still sitting in the garden at Woolsthorpe. He's thinking about Kepler's laws which all work . . . but why should they?

WHY DO PLANETS MOVE IN ELLIPSES? WHY DO THEY MOVE FASTER NEARER THE SUN?

Of course, Isaac knows all about Galileo's constant acceleration idea too, but things falling to the ground was a completely different subject to planets flying about the sun. Isaac had no idea that they might be connected, but someone else in the garden knew. . .

ALICE DROPS A HINT...

Many long seasons had passed since Alice's flight from Grantham Market. Deep within the earth her roots had sprouted and developed, while above in the light her first timid shoot had matured into the trunk from which her branches proudly radiated. Her leaves glowed in the sunshine, collecting the life force to produce green fruit containing her seeds for a future generation.

Gradually Alice became aware of the figure sitting in her shadow, but not through sight or sound. Instead she could feel the heat of concentration, the friction of numbers being twisted on a rack of contradictory thoughts. All that was needed was one pure spark of understanding to ignite the flame of true comprehension. Alice realized she could provide that spark.

From high in her branches, Alice released one of her fruits. She knew of the natural force that would bring it down towards the earth gaining speed with constant acceleration, but would her message be understood?

And so the apple fell.

... AND ISAAC TAKES IT

And so the apple fell.

ADMITTEDLY THE MOON DOESN'T FALL TO EARTH, BUT FAR MORE IMPORTANTLY IT DOESN'T FLY AWAY! AND THAT'S BECAUSE OF THIS INVISIBLE FORCE!

What is Isaac talking about? Look at it like this:

Suppose you have a ball on some string and you spin it around in a circle.

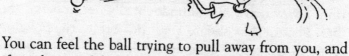

You can feel the ball trying to pull away from you, and if you let go of the string, the ball will fly off.

This is the same as the moon orbiting round the Earth. Just like the ball, it is trying to pull away, but something is holding it in place. Of course the ball is held in its place by the piece of string, but what is holding the moon in place? It must be this invisible force.

AND THIS FORCE IS **GRAVITAS**

So there we are. Of course we call it "gravity" these days, but the invisible pulling power that holds us down had been called GRAVITAS since Aristotle's time. However, even though it had had the same name for thousands of years, Isaac was the first person correctly to understand what it was.

Gravity solved one ancient problem quickly – Aristotle had said that the Earth couldn't be moving or we'd all be thrown off into space. In fact, if it wasn't for gravity, then yes Aristotle would have been right and we would all be thrown off. However, on the surface of Earth, the gravitational force is easily strong enough to hold us on. That's lucky, isn't it?

Another thing Isaac worked out is that the strength of gravity gets a lot weaker as you move further away from Earth.

(Of course that's putting it simply. Isaac used Kepler's third law which you will undoubtedly remember as the one about the square of the orbit time being proportional to the cube of the distance. Isaac made *a simple deduction* and calculated that the strength of gravity obeys an 'inverse square' law. For example, if you had a second moon which was twice as far away from the Earth as the first one, the gravitational force holding the second moon in place would be $\frac{1}{2^2}$ which comes to ¼ of the force holding the first moon. If the second moon was ten times as far away, then the force of gravity would be $\frac{1}{10^2}$ which is ¹⁄₁₀₀. Remember, this all came from *a simple deduction*. It makes you want to scream, doesn't it?)

ISAAC'S UNDISCOVERED DIARY

I have used my ideas about gravity to calculate the way the moon moves, and when I compare my answers with the way the moon actually does move I find them to answer pretty nearly.

> But pretty nearly is not near enough. Why can I not get it to be exact?
>
> Question - where does gravity work from? Is it from the surface of the Earth to the surface of the moon? Or is it from the centre of the Earth to the centre of the moon? The mathematical equations involved are crippling me! ???

You'll have noticed that there aren't millions of Isaac's maths equations all over this page. Sorry if you're disappointed, but as you might imagine, they would give anyone a headache – even Isaac. Unfortunately for him, he wasn't helped by the fact that he didn't have a very accurate measurement of the Earth's diameter to work with and in the end he got so fed up that he abandoned his calculations for quite a few years before he had another go.

Although the gravity idea first occurred to Isaac in Woolsthorpe in 1665, Isaac being Isaac kept very quiet about it. He had to make sure that every detail was perfect and foolproof because the thought that anybody might find the slightest error absolutely freaked him. In the end it took him 20 years to refine and correct everything before he published it all in one of the most famous scientific books of all time – *Principia*.

In the meantime we'll get back to January 1666. Isaac took a short rest from gravity and instead his incredible 12 months of brilliance continued when his brain had. . .

A FLASH OF COLOUR

Although Isaac was still in Woolsthorpe avoiding the plague, he must have popped south at some point because he bought a glass prism – a triangular glass block, all nicely clean and polished – at Stourbridge fair, which was held by the river just outside Cambridge.

Up until that time, it was thought that the different colours were created by mixing darkness and light.

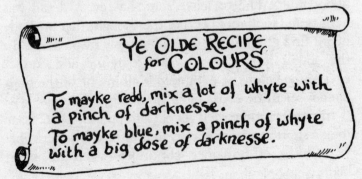

YE OLDE RECIPE
for COLOURS

To mayke redd, mix a lot of whyte with a pinch of darknesse.
To mayke blue, mix a pinch of whyte with a big dose of darknesse.

It was a nice idea, but somehow it didn't hang together. This page you're reading is a mixture of light and darkness, so according to the old theory, if you hold it far away so that the shades blend, the mixture should produce a colour. What do you get?

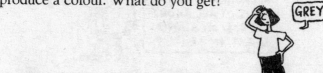

And that's what Isaac thought too.

Already Descartes had tried to analyse a beam of sunlight and produced two colours out of it, red and blue.

OI! HOW ABOUT ME?

Good grief! Who's this?

ROBERT HOOKE. BRILLIANT PHYSICIST AND INVENTOR OF HOOKE'S LAW ABOUT SPRINGS

BA-DOINGGGGGG

This is a book about Isaac Newton, so we'll ignore you.

Anyway, Isaac started to do some experiments on light. . .

Yes, but Isaac suspected that most of it was rubbish.

Yes, but your thinking was based on Descartes who said colours came from just mixing light and darkness, and he also said that light was a sort of pressure which you can feel pushing on the back of the eye. Descartes was all wrong and so were you.

Horrible experiments

Isaac's first experiments with light just used his own eyes. These next bits are pretty gruesome, so brace yourself. . .

Isaac stuck a pointed stick into his eye socket under

his eyeball and wiggled it back as far as it would go. This caused him to see several coloured circles – and he wondered where the colour had come from. (It doubtless also caused him to feel a lot of pain, but he didn't need to wonder where *that* came from!)

Even more dangerous than poking into his own eyes, he spent hours staring directly at the sun to see what effect it would have. The main effect is that he almost blinded himself and had to spend several days in a dark room before his eyesight returned. In those days nobody realized how dangerous the sun could be. Not long before Isaac's time, sailors used a device called 'Jacob's staff' to find out where they were, which involved staring directly into the sun. This led to most sea captains going blind in one eye! These days everybody knows that you must never look at the sun directly, even if you've got sunglasses on, and that poking sticks in your eyes is generally a bad idea.

Once he had recovered, Isaac more sensibly started experiments passing rays of light through his prism.

Maybe you did, but Isaac did it better.

Isaac allowed a thin ray of sunlight to come through a narrow chink in his curtains and hit the prism. The prism bent the ray of light and projected it on to a wall seven metres away. Most importantly, Isaac noticed the light on the wall made a beautiful spectrum showing all the colours of the rainbow.

(If you want to make this book look pretty you could shade these pictures in with coloured pencils.)

Isaac had to think very hard about what he saw. Everybody had thought that white light was pure (in other words it wasn't a mixture of anything) but if that was the case, how had all these colours come from one beam of sunlight?

VIOLET
INDIGO
BLUE
GREEN
YELLOW
ORANGE
RED

With a bit of effort, Isaac realized that white light is not pure at all, it is made up of all the colours of the rainbow put together.

IT IS EACH SEPARATE COLOUR THAT IS PURE, AND WHITE IS THE MIXTURE

Isaac had a lot more experiments to do on light and colours before he was happy with it all, but that would have to wait until he got back to Cambridge.

In the meantime his mind turned back to the problems of the big 'G' and to help him solve them he hit on his next piece of brilliance. . .

THE SECOND MATHS MIRACLE

Just when you thought it was safe to read a bit more, we're about to heave our way through *another* load of calculus! This isn't a very long chapter though, and after it we'll find out about something else horrid that happened in London – just to cheer us all up.

While Isaac was battling out the sums involved with Kepler's laws and Galileo's findings, he realized that he needed to take his 'fluxions' a bit further, and so in May 1666 he invented his method of 'inverse fluxions', which, thanks to Leibniz, we call integral calculus. Although Isaac had to crack a load of even more disgusting sums to work out what to do, in the end it turned out that integral calculus wasn't much harder to do than differential calculus. In fact, it's almost as hard to say the words 'integral and differential calculus' as it is to do it.

Don't worry – if you can't stand the thought of any more maths, luckily this page has a secret trapdoor.

If you go through the trapdoor you'll find you come out behind a completely unexpected picture of Nell Gwyne on page 96, and that way you can miss out on the sums coming up. However, if you're a superbrain keep reading because you'll love this. . .

As we know, differential calculus helped Isaac find the gradients of curves on graphs. This new inverse calculus allowed him to calculate *the area under a curve* which would help him do even fancier calculations about how the moon and planets fly about.

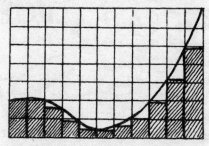

The simple way to get the area underneath a curve is to split it up into very thin rectangles and add them all up. Obviously the thinner the rectangles are, then the better the result, and this is what calculus does.

If you have a curve of $y = x^3$, when we differentiate we would get this: $dy/dx = 3x^2$. (Have a look back at page 61 if you want to be reminded of how we worked this out.)

However, if you wanted to integrate $y = x^3$, it would look like this:

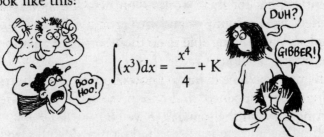

$$\int (x^3)dx = \frac{x^4}{4} + K$$

Don't be put off by the wiggly sign at the front, all we've done is the opposite of differentiating. We've just added a '1' to the little 3 of x^3 to make it into x^4, then divided by the new little number we've got which gives us $x^4/4$. The only odd bit is that sometimes you have to add on an 'integration constant' which we've called K here. K depends on what you are integrating and it's really interesting because. . .

. . .oh all right, integration constants are actually pretty dull unless you're a maths freak so we'll ignore them.

The cool thing about integrating is that if ever you want to check it, you just differentiate and you should get back to where you started. In this case if you differentiate $x^4/4$, you find you get $4x^3/4$ and you can cancel the '4's out to get back to x^3. That irritating K will disappear again in the process which is good news too.

Of course, just working out sums for the sake of it is pointless, but for Isaac working on how the moon and planets were moving – and in particular for studying Kepler's laws – being able to do these sort of calculations was utterly fabulous.

By now you'll be dying to know about the next horrid thing that happened in London, so as a reward for getting through the sums, here we go. . .

A COMPLETELY UNEXPECTED PICTURE OF NELL GWYNE

HOT STUFF IN LONDON

Actually Nell Gwyne isn't what this chapter is about because she hadn't quite got famous yet. At the moment we're dealing with the year 1666 around the time Isaac was inventing his inverse fluxions, and Nell, aged 16, had only just started on her acting career. In three years' time she would become King Charles II's favourite girlfriend, but in the meantime the London newspapers had other hot stuff to keep them busy.

The Stuart Sun

September 1666

CARELESS BAKER COOKS CITY!

The King's baker, Thomas Farrinor, has been named as the man responsible for destroying most of the city of London.

In the evening of 2 September, he had closed his shop in Pudding Lane, but before retiring upstairs, he had failed to ensure his oven fire was safely out. It is suspected that at around midnight some loose sparks landed on a pile of firewood lying near by and within an hour the whole house was in flames.

'It was really smoky,' said his wife. 'And hot too.'

The baker himself managed to escape from an upper window along with his wife, his daughter and a servant, but sadly their maid perished in the flames.

The King has threatened to take the cost of rebuilding London out of the baker's wages.

Why did London go up so easily?

Most of the buildings at the time were built with wooden frames and were covered in 'pitch' which is like a thick black oil, so it only took a few sparks carried by the strong wind blowing that night to set them all ablaze. Soon there were warehouse buildings going up, and they contained barrels holding highly flammable things like oils and brandy which made everything much worse. Within hours of the first careless sparks spitting from the abandoned oven, the Great Fire of London was under way.

The only way to fight fire in those days was to throw buckets of water at it, but this proved pathetic. To stop the fire spreading they realized that they would have to demolish houses in the way, but the city mayor was worried about the rebuilding costs and refused to give the orders. When the King heard about it, he overruled him, but thanks to the delay the fire had the chance to fly right out of control. There was molten lead running down the pavements, and the flagstones themselves were glowing in the heat.

Watching the fire was Samuel Pepys who kept a famous set of diaries, and he noted a particularly sad detail. . .

> *The poor pigeons were loth to leave their houses, but hovered about the windows and balconies, till they some of them burned their wings and fell down...*

Isn't that awful?

Here are some miserable Great Fire facts:

- The Great Fire burned for four days.
- 13,200 houses were burnt down.
- 89 churches were destroyed.
- Thousands of homeless people had to camp out for the winter.
- 10 million pounds of damage was done – equivalent to about 6 billon pounds these days.

Here's an amazing Great Fire fact:

• Only 16 people actually died in the fire itself.

And strange though it may seem, here's one fortunate Great Fire fact:

• The fire probably saved hundreds of lives because it got rid of the rats carrying the plague!

Most of the destroyed buildings were wooden, so at least this gave the city a chance to rebuild itself in stone. The great architect Sir Christopher Wren was signed up, and he designed 49 replacement churches including one of the most magnificent buildings in England, St Paul's Cathedral.

St Paul's replaced the mainly wooden cathedral that stood on the site before. It only took 35 years to build (most decent cathedrals take well over 100 years) and cost £722,799, three shillings, three pennies and one farthing.

The accounts that mention the last little farthing are rather good – especially when you realize that there used to be 960 farthings to a pound. In today's money this is like spending over £350 *million* and still worrying about the last 50p!

As we know, Isaac liked things to be exact. Remember when he first invented the binomial theorem, he calculated numbers to 55 decimal places? He would have loved the fact that this very last farthing was included!

THE SECRET HERETIC

Just before we find out more about Isaac's maths and science stuff, there is another aspect of his studies that we need to know about.

ISAAC'S UNDISCOVERED DIARY

As a natural philosopher I must strive to find the true answers to everything. My maths and science progress well, but I am becoming unhappy with the Bible. The more I study it, the more doubts I have, so I have procured some very early versions in ancient Hebrew which I have translated for myself. It is just as I suspected! It seems that the Holy Trinity of the Father, the Son and the

> Holy Ghost is little more than an invention of scholars down the ages. The Trinity is false, as are many other Christian beliefs. Mankind should be praying directly to the one true God, and yet I fear to announce this conclusion.

Thoughts like this might seem harmless enough to us these days, but at the time it was very dangerous stuff.

• It could have affected Isaac's career because everybody at Cambridge University was supposed to be Christian, and his own college was even called 'Trinity' after the Holy Trinity.
• The country had only just come out of a civil war in which people were killed for the wrong beliefs. The days of burning heretics alive were not far gone.
• What would have worried Isaac even more than losing his job and *even* more than dying, was the fear for his soul if he felt he was not following the true, perfect religion as he saw it.

Not surprisingly, Isaac treated these findings in the same way as all his others. He kept them in a secret notebook and didn't dare tell anyone, although in later life his behaviour started to give him away as we'll see.

BACK TO CAMBRIDGE

When Isaac got back to Cambridge in 1667, although he kept quiet about the other things he'd been discovering, he couldn't resist demonstrating his prism and spectrums. If you think about it, it's a good job he got the prism experiment to work because if he'd insisted that everybody had to stick things in their own eyes to see the effects, the chances are that they would have told him to shut up and go away. As it turned out, in October 1667 he was elected to be a 'fellow' of Trinity College. Being a fellow was quite an honour, as it meant that people were taking him seriously. It also meant that he got paid wages. Not much, but it was better than nothing.

More colour experiments

Isaac himself wanted to check that his colour experiments were foolproof and that his pretty results weren't just being caused by some strange effect of the glass in the prism, so back he went to Stourbridge fair to get some more prisms and do more tests.

- Using some boards with tiny holes in them, he isolated single colours, and then shone them through other prisms to see if he could make these colours change. It turns out he couldn't – for instance a red beam of light remained a red beam of light no matter what he did with it. This meant that the glass in the prisms was not able to change colours or create new colours.

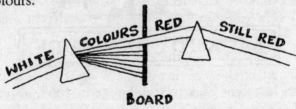

- Using two prisms and a lens, he found that he could split white light into a rainbow, then put the colours back together to make white light again!

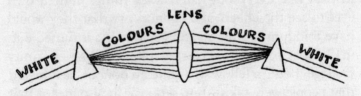

He also worked out how the prism was splitting the white light up. Although all the light was bent as it passed through the prism, different colours were bent by different amounts. The blue light was bent the most, and the red light the least.

This caused Isaac to think about the colours in soap bubbles, and how they occur. He came up with an experiment which involved pushing a glass lens down on to a sheet of glass.

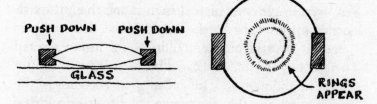

This produces an effect that has become known as 'Newton's Rings' and is a much nicer version of what he was doing when he was poking at the back of his eyes. Newton realized that the colours were caused by light being reflected in the tiny gap between the lens and the glass. (In a soap bubble the colours come from the light being reflected within the very thin wall of the bubble.) As the gap got narrower, so the colour of the light changed.

THIS IS ALL RUBBISH!

Oh no, not you again! Besides, it isn't rubbish, and you'll get your turn later, Mr Hooke.

Isaac's telescope

All Isaac's work on bending light with prisms was to help him come up with a rather useful result.

Some years before, Galileo had taken the credit for inventing the first telescope (although in fact he'd pinched the idea), and after that Kepler had invented a better version. By the 1660s people were starting to use bigger and bigger telescopes to look at the sky: some were over 60 metres high and used massive arrays of lenses.

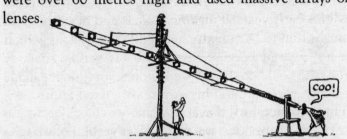

The trouble is that distant stars always looked a bit fuzzy round the edges, and smaller objects only appeared as faint smudges. This is because lenses work by refraction, which means they bend the light as it goes through them. . .

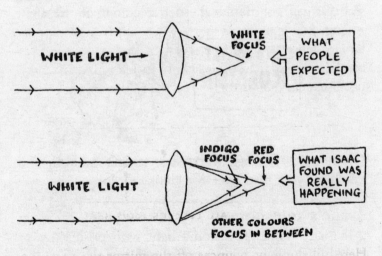

. . .but as Isaac's prisms have shown, when you bend white light, the different colours in it bend by different amounts. Red bends the least and the bluer colours bend the most.

Isaac decided to try and make better telescopes, and it's interesting to note that he did all the work himself. All his early years of making models and machines had taught him to be an extremely skilled craftsman, which is just as well because there probably wasn't anybody else who could do the job well enough for him. He made his own tools, ground his own lenses, fixed up his own stands; in fact, he did everything.

His first thought was that he should try making telescopes with some extra lenses that were specially shaped to cancel out the colour problems, but eventually he realized this was never going to work. Isaac did his usual trick of thinking about it night and day until he hit on the answer – and when he did, it was so brilliant that it revolutionized telescopes for ever.

The problems arose because the light had to pass *through* lenses, but what if the light was made to reflect off them instead? In other words, instead of lenses, why not use a curved mirror?

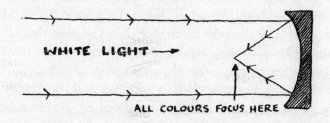

Here, all the light bounces off the mirror together: the colours are not split up at all. To see what the mirror is pointing at you need to look at the point where the light all comes together. Of course, then you have a problem because your head gets in the way.

Isaac's telescope used a small extra mirror so that you could look in from the side without blocking the view.

You might think that the little mirror would show up as a blob in the middle of what you're looking at, but amazingly it doesn't. This is because of the way the large mirror gathers the light and focuses it. All right, that's a bit of a feeble explanation, but understanding the full details of how it works is tougher than chewing through Kepler's laws, so we'll be cowards and leave it.

Since Isaac's time, the mirror has turned out to have another big advantage. When light passes through glass, there's always a little bit that gets absorbed, so the image is slightly darker. This hardly makes any difference if you're looking at things in the daytime, but if you are trying to find very dim objects in the sky at night, this makes life a lot harder. Although Isaac's silver mirrors gave him problems because they got tarnished very easily, these days modern mirrors hardly absorb any light at all so they make star-gazing even easier.

Isaac finished his first reflecting telescope in 1668. It was only 15 cm long and less than 3 cm wide but it made things look more than 30 times bigger. It was more powerful than old 'refracting' telescopes ten times the size.

HANG ON! I MADE THIS REFLECTING TELESCOPE IN 1664, AND IT'S BETTER THAN REFRACTORS 500 TIMES ITS SIZE. I JUST DIDN'T WANT TO TELL ANYBODY.

Yeah, yeah, sure you did.

I KNOW HOW TO FLY TOO, BUT IT'S A SECRET SO DON'T BOTHER ASKING

We weren't going to. Now go away.

'The Newtonian Reflector' was to change Isaac's life. Even if he had shown everybody all his other work, most of it was only numbers on paper and you had to be pretty clever to understand what he had done. What's more, people were bound to offer criticism, which Isaac could not cope with. On the other hand, this powerful little telescope was a gadget that anybody could have fun with and nobody who saw it could deny that it was a pretty smart bit of kit. No wonder Isaac didn't mind showing it off and when he did, the world was impressed.

ISAAC GETS DEAD FAMOUS

In 1668 Isaac was promoted in the university to a 'senior fellow', which meant better wages. For about the only time in his life, he relaxed to celebrate with his friend Wickins. They went to the pub a few times, they gambled at cards and Isaac even changed his image with a posh set of new clothes. This didn't last long though and soon he was back working harder than ever.

By 1669 people had started to realize that Isaac was a bit special. A certain amount of this was due to his old tutor Dr Barrow who did everything he could to promote and encourage Isaac, to the extent that he even gave Isaac his job.

As we know, Dr Barrow had become the 'Lucasian Professor of Mathematics', but in the autumn of 1669, he decided to give it up and concentrate on his religious studies. He insisted that Isaac took his place, which was an extremely generous gesture.

Here's why: although Isaac had managed to get away with his secret religious beliefs as a student, when it came to top jobs such as the Lucasian Professor, you were supposed to be a fully ordained Church of England priest. Dr Barrow himself was extremely religious, but knowing Isaac as well as he did, he must have been aware that Isaac was full of doubt. Many others in his place would have had Isaac kicked out of the university, but instead Barrow did the opposite and insisted to the authorities that it should not be necessary for Isaac to become a priest.

Obviously Barrow would have much preferred it if Isaac had shared his beliefs, but he was big enough to put his personal feelings aside and he even bent the rules a bit to ensure his brilliant young friend got the best academic recognition available. What a nice guy, don't you think?

ISAAC'S UNDISCOVERED DIARY

I knew it was worth sticking with Barrow – I like being the Lucasian Professor! Good wages and lots of free time to follow my own studies. It's almost worth

Isaac's lectures were not a success. Very few students actually wanted to learn anything and although some had turned up at first to enjoy his tricks with prisms, they were soon put off when Isaac started droning on with long and tedious sermons on how he thought everything worked. People used to sneak away and leave him warbling on his own – and it wasn't long before nobody turned up at all and Isaac stood talking to himself. His lectures got shorter and shorter, and fewer and fewer, but as they were part of the job, Isaac talked to empty rooms for almost 20 years.

Despite his boring lectures, Isaac Newton became quite a celebrity in Cambridge, even though he kept very quiet about a lot of what he was up to. In particular, word got out about his telescope and rumours of this 'wondrous instrument' soon reached London.

The Royal Society

This society had been started in London in 1660 and even today it is still going strong. Its full title was 'The Royal Society for the Promotion of Natural Knowledge'.

The society was very keen to know what Isaac was up to and so in December 1671 he let them see his new improved telescope. This one was 20 cm long, 5 cm across and was five times as powerful as his first – and it was an absolute smash hit with everybody, including King Charles II, who asked if he could have a look down it.

Within a month, Isaac was elected to join the Royal Society which cheered him up no end, even if it cost one shilling (which is more than £20 today) a week to be a member.

Almost immediately the secretary of the society, Henry Oldenburg, got Isaac to write out his theories about light and colours, and this was read out to a weekly meeting of the members. It went down a storm with everyone. . .

113

NOT QUITE EVERYONE!

Oh dear. We've forgotten about Robert Hooke. He was the 'Curator of Experiments' of the Royal Society and along with the Bishop of Salisbury and the scientist Robert Boyle, he was asked to check Isaac's findings in detail. Boyle was to become a friend of Isaac's and was a big influence in helping him develop his scientific and even his alchemy skills. Neither he nor the bishop found any fault with Isaac's work, but at the next meeting Hooke gave his reactions.

NEWTON'S STUFF IS RUBBISH! I'VE ALREADY TOLD YOU ABOUT MY EXPERIMENTS TO PRODUCE SPECTRUMS. DESCARTES WAS RIGHT, THERE ARE ONLY TWO PURE COLOURS, SCARLET AND BLUE. ALL THE OTHER COLOURS IN BETWEEN ARE A MIXTURE OF THE TWO. I'VE GOT LOTS AND LOTS OF OTHER THEORIES TOO.

Of course you have Mr Hooke, but your problem is that although your experiments were very good, you didn't understand what the results were telling you.

Hooke's criticisms sent Isaac absolutely beserk, and it wasn't until June that Isaac answered back with a real knockout letter to the society. Put into plain language Isaac said:

I'M SO PLEASED THAT SOMEBODY AS CLEVER AS MR HOOKE CAN'T FIND ANYTHING WRONG WITH MY THEORIES. HE HAS INVENTED SOME RUBBISH AND SAID IT WAS MINE WHEN IT WASN'T, HE HAS TRIED TO SAY THAT SOME OF MY IDEAS ARE REALLY HIS, AND HE HAS IGNORED THE RESULTS OF SOME EXPERIMENTS COMPLETELY.

Hooke got quite a telling-off from the society which shut him up for a bit, but Isaac's theories about light had also caused problems with scientists abroad. One group in particular comprised some English Jesuits (i.e. strong-minded Catholics) living in the Belgian town of Liège, and they had tried to re-create Isaac's experiments but had trouble getting the same results. Although this was because their set-ups were rather different from Isaac's, they argued that Isaac's theories were wrong. He couldn't take it.

In December 1674 Isaac wrote to Henry Oldenburg saying: 'I have determined to concern myself no further about the promotion of philosophy.' Oldenburg was upset by this as he realized that Isaac was one of the society's biggest stars, and tried everything he could think of to stop him leaving.

It's true that Isaac was feeling poor. He thought he was going to lose his well-paid Lucasian Professor job because of his religious beliefs – or disbeliefs to be more accurate. Cambridge was stopping other people from being fellows if they weren't ordained, and so it was looking more and more unfair that Isaac had got away with it. Luckily his friend Isaac Barrow had become the Royal Chaplain at the time, and he suggested to our Isaac that he approached the King for help.

Isaac was dead lucky.

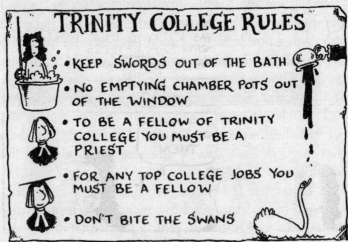

TRINITY COLLEGE RULES

- KEEP SWORDS OUT OF THE BATH
- NO EMPTYING CHAMBER POTS OUT OF THE WINDOW
- TO BE A FELLOW OF TRINITY COLLEGE YOU MUST BE A PRIEST
- FOR ANY TOP COLLEGE JOBS YOU MUST BE A FELLOW
- DON'T BITE THE SWANS

Not only was Barrow able to chat to King Charles II. . .

. . .but Isaac also had a good connection. Do you remember Humphrey Babington? He was brother to Isaac's old landlady Mrs Clark, and when Isaac first started in Cambridge he was Humphrey's sizar. Humphrey was important enough in the college to say:

Isaac softens

Isaac was encouraged by the support he had been given, and he went on to give more details of his experiments with light, including his 'Newton's Rings'. For a time he seemed to get on better with Robert Hooke and asked Henry Oldenburg to remove a remark he had written in one of his papers comparing Hooke to a clown. He even wrote Hooke a letter which said:

What Descartes did was a good step. You have added much several ways, and especially in considering the colours of thin plates. If I have seen further it is by standing on the shoulders of giants.

There, wasn't that a generous thing to say? It looks all nice and friendly, doesn't it? But isn't that a bit strange for our moody, secretive, foul-tempered Isaac?

If you think it looks suspicious, then you might just be right.

Although 'standing on the shoulders of giants' is a great quote (and you'll even find it written around the edge of a £2 coin), you ought to know that Robert Hooke himself was rather stunted and physically deformed. Maybe this remark was Isaac's way of thanking everybody since ancient times, with the one exception of Robert Hooke! In fact Isaac might have deliberately chosen the word "giants" just to be cruel and sarcastic. What do you think?

To give Hooke a bit of credit, if he was upset by this, he never let on. Either way, it wasn't too long before they both fell out again, so there's something for us to look forward to.

In the meantime, Isaac was getting more and more criticism from abroad. Angry letters were going backwards and forwards and Isaac started to suspect the Jesuits in Liège, along with many others, were upsetting him deliberately. It wasn't long before he completely cracked up.

...and by that he meant no more optics work either!

ISAAC'S ODDER OCCUPATIONS

Quite apart from the optical work which had made his name in London, Isaac had still found time to dabble in alchemy at Cambridge. In 1673 he and his friend Wickins moved to some different rooms which had a wooden shed attached to them. It wasn't long before Isaac had lots of mysterious equipment bubbling away inside, and after he had decided to abandon science, he devoted all his time to these stranger studies.

Isaac got very carried away with his alchemy work and you can't blame him. It must have made a nice change from battling through tons of complicated numbers on paper. As he agreed with Isaac Barrow, 'mathematical speculations grow somewhat dry'. He collected well over 100 books on the subject, and if you wanted to print out all the alchemy stuff he wrote himself, it would fill 40 books the size of this one you're reading now.

The good thing about all this alchemy is that it kept Isaac in practice for doing experiments, and it also kept his mind open to different ways of looking at problems.

It's hard to imagine what used to pass through his great brain as he watched all the odd pots bubble away and new crystals, liquids and smells emerge. It's even been suggested that he thought of gravity while doing these bizarre experiments, and that he just made up the story of the falling apple for a laugh.

Fair enough, Isaac. You were the only person there, so we'll have to take your word for it.

The bad thing about Isaac's alchemy is that he used to make all sorts of strange potions which he would try on himself. This was very dangerous because alchemy involved a great deal of work with the 'heavy metals' such as lead and mercury which these days we know to be poisonous. Isaac would be happily breathing in the vapours as he heated them up and even tasting the murky liquids they produced. He even made a joke with Wickins about how drinking 'quicksilver' was turning his hair silver. (It's a good job Isaac was a scientific genius, because a career in comedy wouldn't have lasted long.)

Even worse, some aspects of alchemy were not exactly legal. A few experiments with a chemistry set weren't going to bother anybody, but the really serious alchemists came close to witchcraft. Bearing in mind that Isaac also had his dubious religious beliefs, he had to be very careful about who knew what he was up to.

Possibly the worst outcome of his experiments was due to the hazardous equipment involved, as Isaac found out in March 1668.

One wintery morning, Isaac did something rather odd for him: he went to visit Trinity chapel while some new concoction was heating up. Somehow the flame took hold of the jumble of papers and chemicals strewn around his laboratory, and the whole place nearly burnt down. A massive amount of priceless paperwork was destroyed, which included notes from 20 years of his alchemical experiments, but more importantly a massive book he had written about light was also burnt to ashes. It is thought that this book had been a masterpiece he had been quietly preparing to silence the critics who had upset him so much – and yet in a few minutes, WOOF!, it had all gone up in smoke.

Isaac didn't get over it for ages.

Things got worse. Only the previous year he had lost two important friends when both Barrow and Oldenburg had died. Now, in 1679, Isaac had to rush up to Lincolnshire to look after his mother who had come down with a bad fever. Despite all his medicines and round the clock attention, she died in June leaving him upset and confused. To frustrate him even more, he had to stay until the end of the year to sort out the family business and collect a lot of money they were owed. To take his mind off his troubles, he started to think again about the invisible force that made the apple fall, but funnily enough, it was thanks to his old enemy that he really started to make his breakthrough.

ISAAC GETS A KICK-START

When Isaac got back to Cambridge in December 1679, he found a letter from Robert Hooke waiting for him.

THE SECRETARY OF THE ROYAL SOCIETY IS NOW ME, SO THERE!

Hooke had been thinking about the movements of the planets, and other people in the Royal Society had encouraged him to see if Isaac could provide some mathematical answers. To encourage Isaac, Hooke promised that anything he sent would not be made public.

Isaac didn't want to be bothered with Hooke, but so as not to offend the society, he sent a little 'fancy' he had had about how things fall out of tall buildings. (Because the Earth is spinning round, they don't quite fall straight down. Isaac said they fell in a neat little spiral.) As it turns out, Isaac should have sat on it.

By a lucky guess, Hooke had indeed stumbled across a flaw in Isaac's little fancy and showed that things fall in an *elliptical* spiral. He was so smug about this that he went back on his promise and told *everybody*.

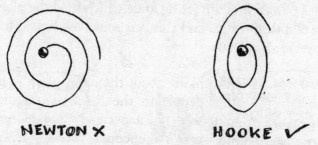

At first Isaac tried to ignore it, but Hooke rubbed it in as much as he could and had a big laugh about it with all his mates down in London.

Isaac didn't contact anyone for a year. Was he. . .

- sulking?
- plotting his revenge?
- suddenly aware of something totally awesome?

It was a combination of all three. Because of gravity and the Earth spinning round, it seemed that Hooke was right and objects *did* fall in an elliptical pattern.

Ellipses! Where have we seen those before?

PLANETS FLYING ROUND THE SUN OF COURSE!

Other people in the society were starting to miss Isaac's contributions, so they got Hooke to try and patch things up by sending some chatty scientific letters hoping for a response. In January 1680, one of these brought up the idea of a central attracting force which held the planets in elliptical orbits, and this was somehow linked to an inverse square law.

INVERSE SQUARE LAW? BUT THAT'S HOW GRAVITY BEHAVES! I FOUND OUT WHEN I DID SOME SUMS ON KEPLER'S THIRD LAW!

GLAD IT CAME IN HANDY

R.I.P JOHANNES KEPLER 1571-1630

Up to this point, the only gravity Isaac had thought about was when things were attracted down to Earth. But suppose the sun also attracted things by gravity? Maybe gravity could work at long range and reach right across space and hold the planets in their elliptical orbits?

Wa-hey!

Hooke had reached a few conclusions of his own about gravity (which in typical Hooke style were based on guesswork with no proof), but he didn't have the vision to see what they were all leading up to. Even if he had managed to see the big picture, he couldn't possibly have done the maths to tie it all up, but Isaac could. And he did.

THREE BLOKES HAVE A COFFEE

These days in London, if you want a small business meeting or a private chat or even to do a sneaky deal, you might meet up in a wine bar or restaurant. It's jollier and more intimate than being in an office or a conference room, so people tend to talk more and find it easier to agree on things.

In the 1680s people used coffee shops for the same reason. In the warmth and the smoke and the smell, all sorts of deals were struck and anything from art to assassinations was discussed.

And so it was that in one of these coffee shops in the new year of 1684 one particular meeting took place between three men.

There was Christopher Wren, who is best remembered as the architect who designed St Paul's Cathedral, but who was also infuriatingly good at everything else.

There was Robert Hooke. We've seen enough of him already, don't you think?

128

Then there was Edmund Halley, a gentleman who is best known for predicting that "Halley's Comet" would return to our skies every 76 years. It was an awesome calculation  when you bear in mind that he only ever saw it go past once!

The conversation got on to the subject of gravity.

129

Halley wasn't impressed with Hooke, so instead he paid Isaac a surprise visit and asked him very nicely if he could help. Isaac told him about the sums he had already done on inverse square laws and how they explained the planets travelling in elliptical orbits. Halley was over the moon, especially when Isaac offered to dig out his notes and show him.

Unfortunately, Isaac then claimed he couldn't find what Halley wanted, but said he would write it all out again. Halley came away wondering if Isaac was just being his usual secretive self, but all he could do was wait quietly and hope something would turn up. To his relief, a few months later nine pieces of paper arrived at Halley's house. They were called: 'De Motu Corporum In Gyrum' which is Latin for 'About the Motion of Orbiting Bodies'.

Halley's good manners and patience had rewarded him with a scientific jackpot.

THE END OF ETHER

A little chapter in which Isaac completely trashes yet another accepted fact of science.

As he was preparing the 'De Motu' papers for Halley, Isaac had a few other problems to solve. One of them concerned 'ether' which everybody thought existed, but which didn't fit in with Isaac's sums at all. So what was (or wasn't) ether? Well, it came about like this. . .

When earlier scientists tried to explain their version of things like light and magnetism, they didn't like the idea that anything could travel across nothing.

They felt that there must be something through which things like light and magnetism travel, and they called this something the 'ether'.

Ether was supposed to be like a very light gas which could pass through everything, and they did an experiment 'proving' it existed.

They knew that if they started a normal pendulum swinging, it would stop in a few minutes. They thought it was because the moving pendulum was having to push against the air and also this 'ether' which eventually slowed it down. They then tried a pendulum in a glass case from which all the air had been sucked out. The pendulum took hours to stop – but finally it did. They decided this was because it was still having to push against the ether which was everywhere – even inside the case.

It seemed they had proved that ether existed.

However, when Isaac started doing his sums about the planets moving in orbit, all the calculations worked out perfectly – providing nothing was slowing the planets down. This indicated that there was no ether after all.

Isaac then did the pendulum experiment again, but his version. He made a hollow pendulum, put it in the glass case, sucked the air out, set it going and then timed how long it took to stop.

Next Isaac filled up the pendulum with sand.

Isaac then tried filling the pendulum with other things like mercury or oil and, each time, he put it in the case, pumped all the air out, set it off and timed it. The result was always the same. Whatever it was that was bringing the pendulum to a halt, Isaac was convinced of one thing. . .

To conventional scientists this was impossible because it meant that force could pass through empty space. However, Isaac wasn't scared to take on new ideas (which included pushing alchemy and religion to their limits), so as magical as it seemed, 'no ether' was the only answer.

ISAAC'S NEW SUPPORT TEAM

Isaac had never had a lot of close chums, and in 1683 even John Wickins had moved on. Although they had shared rooms for 20 years, they were hardly ever in contact again. Maybe the devout Christian Wickins had finally had enough of Isaac's strange religious views, or maybe Isaac had got fed up sharing with someone who worshipped what he had decided were heathen images. Maybe it was just that Wickins had had enough of all Isaac's weird experiments and anti-social behaviour. Whatever it was, he went.

Isaac suddenly found he needed someone else to do all the boring jobs that Wickins had been kindly doing for all those years.

WANTED

Laboratory Assistant to work with strange bad-tempered genius. Extremely long hours, little sleep, dangerous equipment and minimal holidays. Good handwriting essential.

In the end Isaac took on an assistant called Humphrey Newton who also came from Lincolnshire but wasn't any relation.

More importantly, the time had come for Isaac's work to reach a wider audience, and it needed exactly the right person to coax it out of him and then present it to the world at large. Edmund Halley had arrived on the scene just at the right time.

When Halley first got the 'De Motu' papers, he was so thrilled that he rushed back to Cambridge to see if Isaac had any more interesting papers that nobody else had seen. Of course, he had tons of them and Halley offered to pay to have them all published.

It was a very generous offer from Halley, but Isaac didn't want to take it up just yet. While he had been preparing the 'De Motu' papers, something awesome had occurred to him. . .

If the sun has gravity, and the Earth has gravity, does *everything* have gravity? This was to lead to his theory of 'universal gravitation' – or in other words Isaac had started to understand the real implications of the big 'G'.

It's important to realize that although we've nicknamed gravity "the big G" for fun, if Isaac had called it "the big G" he might have been thinking of something else. This invisible force that worked right through everything in the universe – could this be the evidence of God that he had been looking for? God was supposed to be invisible, powerful and "omnipresent" (which means everywhere) just like gravity! Best of all, even though he could see the effects of gravity on everything around him, it was impossible to explain why it was there or how it worked. Gravity was as majestic and mysterious as God!

Isaac was extremely excited by this thought, but in the meantime he decided he would put all the solid facts he had together. If they were all going to be published, he wanted the result to be awesome. And it was.

THE BIG BIG BOOK OF SCIENCE

Isaac worked on his great book solidly for a year and a half. Most of the time he was shut in his rooms and his only company was Humphrey, who meticulously wrote the book out word for word.

During the early months Newton kept sending notes to John Flamsteed, the Astronomer Royal, pestering him for the most accurate readings possible on the positions of the planets. Flamsteed went out of his way to help as much as he could, although for the life of him he couldn't fathom why Isaac was being so fussy. Like everybody else, he thought that the orbits of the planets were fixed by the sun's gravity and that was it. He could not imagine what Isaac had begun to suspect, that each planet had its own gravity and in a very tiny way they were affecting each other's paths.

Finally, in summer 1686, *Philosophiae Naturalis Principia Mathematica* was ready. Isaac knew it was going to be a monster classic, so he took great care to make sure it looked like one.

How to write a 17th century monster classic

- Write it in Latin. This is so that any academic in the world will be able to read it. It also means that ignorant peasants won't understand a single word, which stops them asking you stupid questions about it.
- Don't use any calculus. After all, you're still trying to keep your new maths method secret. Instead, all your proofs and reasoning should be based on ancient Greek maths. It makes life a lot harder, but at least everybody has been used to it for thousands of years.
- Give it a fancy title which means 'Mathematical Principles of Natural Philosophy'.
- Don't let Robert Hooke see it.

Isaac certainly got the first three points right, but as we're about to find out, he messed up with the last one.

By the time Isaac had finished writing it, the *Principia* (as it was commonly called) ended up being not just one book, but three. The first book was basically his 'De Motu' papers reworked and in April 1686 a handwritten copy was presented to the Royal Society. Edmund Halley took charge of it and it's a good job he did because without him it would never have been published. Halley abandoned his own work to make the time to encourage Isaac and check what he'd written. He paid all the expenses, and he also had two big problems to deal with.

Halley's publishing problems

The first problem is that publishing books costs a lot of money, and it is always a gamble whether or not a book will earn it back. (Incidentally, if you bought this book with your own money, this seems a good point to thank you. So thank you.) The society had only just paid out to publish a rather grand book called *De Historia Piscium* but it had hardly sold any copies. It's surprising really when you discover that translated from Latin, the title is the extremely groovy *The History of Fishes*. You'd think that would have been a runaway best-seller, wouldn't you? Still, that's the book trade for you.

Anyway, the society members were all feeling a bit dubious about shoving their remaining funds into another book, and it took a lot of cajoling from Edmund Halley – not to mention a lot of his own money – to make them do it. It has to be said that when it was first published, the *Principia* didn't sell too many either, but eventually it became essential reading all over the world.

Halley's other problem was that he had to deal with a very angry complaint.

TOO RIGHT I'M ANGRY! NEWTON'S PINCHED MY IDEAS ON GRAVITY!

OK, Mr Hooke, let's try and be fair about this. A few years earlier you wrote your *Discourse on the Nature of Comets* and yes, you did say that all the planets and the sun have their own gravities, and you did mention an inverse square law, BUT your explanations were feeble and relied on 'ether', which doesn't exist. The fact is that Isaac had worked out the inverse square law properly ages before you, even if he did keep it secret. In the meantime you were just guessing and couldn't prove a thing.

I COULD PROVE IT IF I WANTED TO, BUT I JUST CAN'T BE BOTHERED

Yeah, yeah, sure you can.

LOOK ISAAC, MAYBE YOU COULD JUST SAY ROBERT HOOKE HELPED YOU A TINY BIT? THE POOR MAN HAS BECOME REALLY ILL, YOU KNOW

SERVES HIM RIGHT. AND I'M CROSSING OUT EVERY TRACE OF HIS NAME!

Later in 1686 Isaac finished the second book, but as he came to finish the last one he heard that Hooke was still rubbishing him to anybody in the London coffee shops who would listen. To Halley's utter disappointment Isaac refused to release the third book.

In the end Halley got Christopher Wren to convince Isaac that all Hooke was managing to do was make himself look even more objectionable and stupid than ever. Isaac changed his mind, but before he released the third book, he rewrote it. He had tried to make the original version easy to follow, but now he arranged it so that you could only understand it if you had read the first two. He also made the maths as complicated as possible, just to make sure that Hooke had no chance of following it, or worse still claiming it was his.

So what was the *Principia* all about?
Forces.

There, that was simple wasn't it?

Actually, the *Principia* was 550 pages long so there was a bit more detail than that, but if you're lying in the bath while you read this and the water is starting to get a bit cold, here are the two main things it says:

- The harder you push something, the faster it speeds up.
- Everything is attracted to everything else, and the bigger and solider and closer they are, the more the attraction.

Right then, if you want to pull out the plug and get dried off, then away you go. When you get back to this book you can even cheat and start from page 158, but if you do that you'll miss out on the brilliant technical bits which the rest of us are going to play with now. It's your loss.

The technical bits – made nice and simple

The ideas of force and gravity and weight are all simple enough to us these days, but before Isaac introduced them the world was only used to 'ether' and 'things assuming their rightful place'. Not only was Isaac supplying these amazing new ideas, he was showing how everything could be measured and calculated rather than just vaguely saying 'it happens'.

The most useful parts of the *Principia* are still used by engineers and physicists every single day, and they are:

NEWTON'S LAWS OF MOTION

Newton's First Law: Everything stays still, or keeps moving in a straight line at the same speed, unless a force makes it change.

Well, the first bit of this is simple enough. Anything that isn't moving won't move until something gives it a shove. Easy.

The second bit is more interesting. It says that anything moving will keep moving in a straight line at the same speed for ever unless a force acts on it. Imagine you are riding in a car at a steady speed on a smooth straight road. If you shut your eyes and block your ears, you will not be able to tell how fast you are moving – you might not even know if you have stopped. That's because there are no forces acting on you and you can just sit comfortably in your seat.

If the car suddenly starts speeding up, you would know because you feel yourself getting pushed back into your seat by the force acting on you. Of course, once the car has reached the faster speed, it stops speeding up, so you don't feel the force any more.

If the car suddenly brakes, the speed quickly slows down and you would feel yourself being thrown forward. That's why you need a seat-belt, to provide the force needed to slow you down.

SPEEDING UP...   **... BRAKING**

If the car takes a few corners, you also feel it because you get thrown over to one side or the other by the forces involved.

If you go on a 'white knuckle' roller-coaster, it speeds you up, slows you down, and pushes you through corners not only sideways but also vertically (in other words it does loop-the-loops). This means that you feel massive amounts of force coming at you from all different directions, and that's what makes it so exciting!

WAHOO!

So: for speeding up, slowing down or turning a corner, there is always a force involved. That's Newton's First Law.

There's one more interesting thought about this:

If you throw a ball straight out in front of you, as it flies away two forces will be acting on it. Air resistance will gradually slow the ball down, and at the same time gravity will pull the ball down towards the ground.

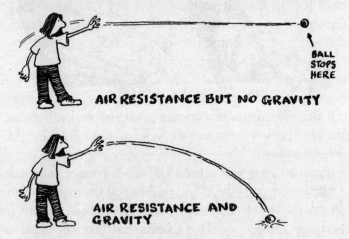

BALL STOPS HERE

AIR RESISTANCE BUT NO GRAVITY

AIR RESISTANCE AND GRAVITY

If it wasn't for these forces, then your ball could fly off in a straight line all the way to the end of the universe!

!?

NO AIR RESISTANCE AND NO GRAVITY

Good one, eh?

Newton's Second Law: The change in motion depends on how strong the force is.

Have you ever tried to push a car by yourself? At first to get it moving you have to push really hard. This is because the car is building up speed, or in other words it is accelerating – which uses force. Once the car is up to the speed you want, you don't need to push nearly as hard just to keep it going. (Once the car is going fast enough, the only force you need is to push the air out of the way and overcome the friction of the wheels.)

If you have another person to help, then the car will receive twice as much force – and you will find it will build up speed twice as fast. On the other hand, if you are pushing two cars, then they will only speed up half as fast.

POSITIONS AFTER 10 SECONDS

There's a formula for this law which is probably the most important formula in physics:

Force = Mass × Acceleration
or **F = MA** for short.

Of course it's a bit mean writing something like 'force equals mass times acceleration' without explaining it, and so in the first part of the *Principia* Isaac took great care to say exactly what each word meant. Let's find out for ourselves:

ACCELERATION
We've already seen what this is when we found out about Galileo. In case you can't be bothered to turn the pages back, it's how fast your speed is changing. Suppose you set off travelling at 1 metre per second, then a second later you're going at 2 metres per second, and then a second after that you're going at 3 metres per second. . . You'll see your speed is getting faster by 1 metre per second every second. Rather confusingly this would be called 1 metre per second per second. You can even write it as $1ms^{-2}$, but this is all getting a bit complicated so let's hurry on. . .

MASS (and how to lose weight the easy way!)
These days mass is measured in kilograms. It depends on the volume of an object and its density, or, put more simply, how big a thing is and how solid it is.

Suppose you have a brick and sponge that are the same size. The brick will have a much greater mass, because it is more dense. Of course if your sponge was

1,000 times bigger than the brick then it would be heavier, because there's so much more of it.

The odd thing about mass is that it is *not* the same as weight. You can test this for yourself, with just some bathroom scales and a space rocket. Here's what to do.

1 Get some bathroom scales, stand on them and see what your weight is – e.g. 50 kg.

2 Take your bathroom scales and get in the rocket and fly to the moon.

3 When you have landed on the moon, get on the scales again. You will find your weight is about 8 kg. *Gosh!*

4 Set off home in the rocket, but while you are in space try and get on the scales. This will be tricky because you will be floating about, and of course your weight will be zero!

So what has happened? Why has your weight got less? Has somebody scooped out all your insides with a spoon?

Of course not. The hard bit to understand is that weight is a force. When you stand on the scales, they don't actually measure your mass, they measure the force of your feet pushing down. This force comes from the Earth's gravity pulling your mass towards the ground. On the moon there is a lot less gravity pulling your mass down, so the scales show less force. In deep space there is almost no gravity at all, so the scales don't show any force – in other words you are weightless! However, your MASS is the same – you are still 50 kg.

Because the bathroom scales are measuring a force rather than mass, they shouldn't really be marked in kilograms, they should be marked in units of force – but what is force measured in, eh? Let's see. . .

FORCE
Before Isaac explained force, nobody was even sure what it was, but these days we know exactly.

Suppose you have a lump of metal with a mass of 1 kg floating in space. Now suppose you give it a steady push so that it accelerates at a rate of 1 metre per second every second. Guess how much force you need to apply? The answer is . . . 1 Newton.

Yes, when they invented metric units, in honour of Isaac's work they called units of force after him. So to be really accurate, your bathroom scales should be marked in Newtons. So is 1 Newton the same as the weight of 1 kg? Sadly, no. . .

Let's get back to **Force = Mass × Acceleration**.

Galileo showed that a falling object has a constant acceleration, and on Earth this has been measured to be about 10 metres per second per second. (On the moon it's only about 1.6 metres per second per second.) So if we put the acceleration to equal 10 in the equation, we can work out the force of an object falling to Earth:

Force = Mass × 10

So if your mass is 50 kg, if you fell out of a building the force pulling you to Earth would be:

Force = 50 × 10 which comes to 500 Newtons.

Because the acceleration is constant, that means this force is the same whatever speed you are falling at. Even if you are falling at zero speed (i.e. not falling at all, but just standing on your bathroom scales), the force pulling you down to the ground is still 500 Newtons.

That's why your bathroom scales should really be marked in Newtons rather than kilograms. However, the people that make bathroom scales assume that you will only be using them on Earth, so they get away with marking them in kilograms.

At the start of this book, you were told you'd find out why too many Newtons would kill you – well, if a two-tonne elephant sat on you, it would be pushing down with a force of 20,000 Newtons. Nasty!

Newton's Third Law: For every action there is an equal and opposite reaction.

This one is nice and simple. All it means is if you push against something, it pushes back. (Or if you pull, it pulls back.) It's the same as if you are in a car which is speeding up, the back of the seat is trying to push you forward, and at the same time your body is pushing back into the seat. Let's look at another example, two tug-of-war teams pulling on a rope.

If they both pull with the same force, they don't go anywhere.

If one team pulls slightly harder, the extra force causes the other team to accelerate towards them.

However, if the other team suddenly let go of the rope, the first team don't have anything to pull against so they all fall over.

Another way of looking at this is to see what happens when you jump in the air. As you push your feet against the ground, the ground pushes back and causes you to go up to a height of, say, 1 metre. However, your feet pushing against the ground also cause the Earth to move in the opposite way from you. Because the Earth is a lot bigger and heavier than you, it only moves a tiny bit. Actually it's a VERY tiny bit, about 0.000000000000000000000001 of a metre.

You might be worried that you've knocked the Earth out of orbit, but don't panic. As you come back down, the opposite thing happens. Although the Earth is pulling you towards it, you are also pulling the Earth back towards you. After your jump, the Earth will be back in the same place! Of course, if you jump so high that you shoot right off the Earth, then yes, you will have budged it over ever so slightly. Mind you, as you've ended up flying round space on your own, and you've probably forgotten to take any sandwiches or a thick jumper, the Earth being slightly out of position will be the least of your problems.

The big 'G' formula

All these laws and descriptions started to lead up to one dazzling grand finale. Isaac said that everything from the tiniest particle to the biggest star had its own gravity, and so everything was attracted to everything else. But how powerful was this attraction? Isaac came up with this formula which gives the attraction between any two objects:

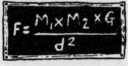

$$F = \frac{M_1 \times M_2 \times G}{d^2}$$

F means the force (obviously).
M_1 is the mass of the first object.
M_2 is the mass of the second object.
d is the distance between them.
G is a fixed number called the gravitational constant.

Isaac claimed his formula applied to absolutely everything of every size in the whole universe, and called it his Universal Law of Gravity.

SEE THAT? THAT'S GRAVITY. THAT IS...

Actually, at the time he was making a bit of a big-headed guess in claiming this, but since then he has been proved right. This formula fitted in with Kepler's laws, it fitted in with the observations Flamsteed had provided from the Royal Observatory, and it smashed open the barriers to solving all sorts of problems.

- For a planet going round the sun, you just fill in the masses of the planet and the sun, work out the distance and then you can calculate the force holding them together.

- If you wanted to calculate the force of gravity on a rocket leaving the Earth, just fill in the masses of the rocket and Earth, and then keep changing the distance as it gets further away. You can also use some of Isaac's calculus for this.

- You could use it to redraw the numbers on bathroom scales so that they would work properly on the moon.

- It explains why pendulum clocks run slightly slower at the Equator than the North pole. Because the Earth spins round, it tends to bulge out a bit at the sides, which means that a clock on the Equator is ever so slightly further away from the centre of the Earth. This means that gravity on the Equator is a tiny bit weaker!

- If you are sitting across the room from somebody you really fancy, you can even calculate the gravitational attraction between you both! We'll see how to do that in a minute.

Isaac had made a massive breakthrough. The only thing he never lived to see was an accurate value for the number 'G'. It was finally worked out in 1798 by Henry Cavendish, and depends on what you measure everything in. If your distance is in metres, your masses are in kilograms and your force is in Newtons (of course!), then G= 0.0000000000667.

So there you are in a room sitting 3 metres away from the most fanciable person in the whole world. What is the gravitational force pulling you together?

Let's say you both weigh 50 kg. Use the formula. . .

$$F = \frac{M_1 \times M_2 \times G}{d^2}$$

Put in the numbers. . .

$$F = \frac{50 \times 50 \times 0.0000000000667}{3 \times 3}$$

. . .and you'll find that the force pulling you together is 0.0000000185 Newtons.

To be honest, this isn't quite enough to drag you screaming across the room into a frenzied collision of passion, but if you were both floating in a vacuum and were prepared to wait a couple of days you should eventually drift together. Every little helps, don't you think?

MEANWHILE ON THE THRONE...

While Isaac was writing the *Principia*, all sorts of trouble had been brewing around him. As was often the case in those days, it was mainly caused by different monarchs coming and going and bringing different religions with them. The start of this confusion dates back to Henry VIII.

BACK IN 1532...

I WANT A DIVORCE FROM MY FIRST WIFE CATHERINE SO I CAN MARRY ANNE BOLEYN. AS WE ARE ALL ROMAN CATHOLICS, I'LL HAVE TO ASK THE POPE.

ULP...

SORRY, BUT THE POPE REFUSES. KING CHARLES OF SPAIN WON'T LET HIM. CATHERINE IS CHARLIE'S AUNTIE, YOU KNOW.

And so Henry VIII got rid of the Pope as head of the Church in England, which led to a Protestant monarchy. Then it all got very complicated. Here's how it went:

HENRY VIII	1502-1547	CATHOLIC BUT THEN BECAME HEAD OF THE CHURCH OF ENGLAND	
EDWARD VI	1547-1553	PROTESTANT	BETWEEN 1649 AND 1660 THE FANATICAL PROTESTANT CROMWELL WAS IN CHARGE.
'BLOODY' MARY	1553-1558	ABSOLUTELY SCREAMING CATHOLIC	
ELIZABETH I	1558-1603	SERIOUSLY PROTESTANT	
JAMES I	1603-1625	GOT TALKED INTO BEING PROTESTANT	
CHARLES I	1625-1649	PROTESTANT	
CHARLES II	1660-1685	PROTESTANT, BUT SECRETLY CONVERTED TO CATHOLICISM ON HIS DEATHBED	NOTE:

Life could be tricky, especially in Mary or Elizabeth's time, because you could be burnt alive for going to the wrong sort of service.

Anyway, in our story we've reached the year 1685 and everybody has just about got used to having a Protestant on the throne when suddenly. . .

The Stuart Sun

February 1685

KING CONKS OUT

Last week in Whitehall, King Charles II suffered a stroke and after five days in bed finally passed away on 6 February.

It is rumoured that in his last hours he requested a visit from his old friend Father Huddlestone, who converted the dying monarch to the Catholic Church in his final minutes.

This is not altogether unexpected as Charles's grand-mother Anne (wife of King James I) was always a strong Catholic, as is his brother who automatically becomes the new King James II. The new king is 51.

CROMWELL STILL STUCK UP

Yes folks, after almost 20 years, Oliver Cromwell's head can still be seen on a pole outside Westminster Hall – although he's now encrusted with bird droppings, and the eyeballs have long since been pecked out.

160

The new King James was clever and businesslike but most of all he was keen to see England become a strongly Catholic country again. He used threats to see that Catholics quickly got top jobs in the army, the legal profession, the government, and the universities. This did not go down well, especially in Cambridge.

Isaac nearly gets himself hanged

Isaac had never cared much for the Church of England, but he hated the Catholic Church of Rome far more. Despite the fact that he would have been stupid to draw attention to his own views on religion, he had the nerve to speak out against the new king, and he became heavily involved in the Cambridge resistance. This was extremely dangerous. Early in James's reign 300 rebels had been sentenced to the gallows by Judge Jeffreys at the 'Bloody Assizes', and the way Isaac was behaving it wouldn't have been long until his turn came.

The king that ran away

Luckily most of the country thought that James was behaving unfairly and they quickly got fed up with him. In 1688, the Protestant William of Orange took advantage of this and sailed over with an army from Holland.

161

The Stuart Sun

December 1688

NO KING? YOU'RE JO-KING!

Locals cheered as Dutch William marched on London expecting a fight from James II, but were disappointed when the King failed to show. It seems that rather than face the anger of the mob, not to mention William's Protestant army, the King has fled. No wonder, he must have remembered that his father King Charles I was executed by Oliver Cromwell. Doubtless James didn't fancy the same treatment!

When William was asked if he would be pursuing King James to bring him to trial, he replied 'Uh?' It seems that William does not speak English.

In fact, James flitted about a bit, and after a few months in France he decided to try and get back into England from Ireland, hoping the local Catholics would help him. In the end William took an army over to get him at Dublin, but James quickly ran back to France again, this time for good. William didn't go after him, and no wonder! Luckily for James, William had married his daughter Mary and it would have been a bit awkward for William to explain to his wife that he might need to execute her father.

William and Mary jointly took the throne in 1689, which was a bit of a result for Isaac, in that he was invited to join parliament as MP for Cambridge University. Mind you, he only made one speech. . .

AT LAST SOME NEW FRIENDS

Isaac was only an MP for a year, but during his time in London he attracted a gang of useful friends. Here are some of them:

John Locke – philosopher

Locke had been hiding abroad during the trouble and he had read the *Principia*, although he freely admitted he didn't understand any of the maths. Locke did a great deal to publicize Isaac's brilliant work, and even got Isaac to simplify his explanations of gravity. The two of them got to be such close friends that Isaac even confided his religious views to him. Locke arranged to have them published in Holland, but at the last minute Isaac lost his nerve.

Christopher Wren – all-round clever type

We've come across Wren before, top architect, mathematician, and generally a neat guy to hang out with. At the time he was busy rebuilding most of London, including St Paul's Cathedral.

Samuel Pepys – diary keeper

Yes, we've come across him too. He's most famous for keeping a very good (and in some parts very rude) diary of his day-to-day life in London. He also managed to get himself some pretty good jobs, including a few years as president of the Royal Society.

Charles Montague – useful contact

Montague was a jolly chum who became Lord Halifax, and then the Chancellor of the Exchequer. He wasn't too concerned about Isaac's work, but he was good company to have around and would prove to be useful later on.

King William III – king

He was the king, obviously, which made him pretty handy to know.

Nicholas Fatio de Duillier – Swiss mathematician

'Fatio' as he gets called for short was over 20 years younger than Isaac and probably the most interesting of the gang. In his early twenties he was rated as a sharp brain himself, and he managed to mix with all sorts of clever types including the German Leibniz. In 1689 he got himself a job touring England with the great Dutch academic Christiaan Huygens and that was how he came to meet Isaac at the Royal Society.

Fatio hero-worshipped the top academics, and in particular he thought Isaac was great. In return Isaac was very taken by this clever and keen young man, and the two of them became very close friends. Maybe Isaac saw Fatio as the son he might have wished to have had, or maybe Isaac was just flattered that his work had made an impact on someone so clever from a younger generation. Whatever it was, they met up whenever they could and wrote extremely fond letters to each other when they were apart. Maybe they rather fancied each other, but if that was the case then you could be sure that Hooke would have had some snide remarks to make.

SNIDE REMARKS
TO MAKE
ABOUT WHAT?

There you are: if Hooke didn't pick up on it, then there can't have been much in it.

Dark and dangerous studies

Fatio had brought some odd ideas with him, and encouraged Isaac to get deeper and deeper into the spookier side of his investigations. After the success of the *Principia*, Isaac was trying to follow it up with something even better that would bring alchemy and religion all in line in the same way as he had sorted out gravity. He would have loved to publish a book saying that the Christian way of following God was all wrong, and to be able to prove it absolutely with maths and science. Of course, unless he could find that absolute proof he would be branded as a heretic, so these studies had to be as secret as ever. They were also every bit as dangerous – he even had another big fire in his laboratory when his dog Diamond knocked over a candle.

His friendship with Fatio didn't last. Fatio wrote to Isaac in 1692 saying he was dying, which panicked Isaac a lot, but actually Fatio lived for another 60 years so he can't have been that bad. Maybe Fatio's problem was that although Isaac had time for him, most of the other academics had started to think both him and his work were a bit of a joke.

Oh look! It's Newton's Baboon!

After another year of letters and visits, they lost contact. Fatio disappeared and eventually turned up living with an extremely occult and disturbing French religious sect.

Isaac gets ill and better again

Fatio had not only idolized Isaac, he had encouraged him with his investigations of the darkest and most dangerous subjects. When he went, Isaac had not only lost his fondest friend, he had also lost his inspiration and the nerve he needed to carry on his work. Of course without his work, Isaac had nothing.

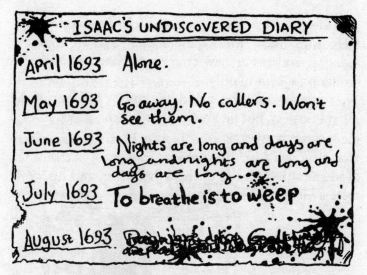

ISAAC'S UNDISCOVERED DIARY

April 1693 Alone.

May 1693 Go away. No callers. Won't see them.

June 1693 Nights are long and days are long and nights are long and days are long...

July 1693 To breathe is to weep

August 1693 [obscured by ink blots]

Now then, we've reached a rather important point in this book because after this Isaac doesn't do any more maths or science. Yippee! You're probably thinking that we haven't any more equations or complicated bits to battle through. In fact, you're tempted to have a quick flick through to the end of the book to check, aren't you? Go on, you know you want to. We'll wait for you. . .

. . .Hello! Welcome back. OK, there are one or two more ugly looking bits right at the end, but as they aren't Isaac's we aren't going to make too much of a song and dance about them. Instead, let's just find out how he became even meaner and horrider than he already was, so back we go to 1693.

It wasn't until September that Isaac started making contact with his London friends again, and when he did he sent some rather strange and unpleasant letters. Pepys and Locke both got one, and they had the sense to realize that Isaac was seriously ill. They got together and after a lot of effort they convinced Isaac to let them help him. Isaac took their advice to join them in London and get a new start, but what was there in London for him to do?

He was asked if he would like to be president of the Royal Society, but he absolutely refused. . .

BECAUSE I WAS STILL THE SECRETARY

However, he got another extremely kind offer. His old friend Charles Montague had just been given the job of Chancellor of the Exchequer, and one of his departments was the Royal Mint, where all the coins were made. Montague offered Isaac the job of 'Warden of the Mint'.

THE FORGER'S NIGHTMARE

Montague's offer was intended to be an act of charity. Along with Isaac's other friends, he realized how much science owed to Isaac and his findings, and he couldn't bear the thought of Isaac spending the rest of his days rotting away in poverty (like Johannes Kepler did). There's also a suggestion that Montague had been rather struck by Isaac's niece Catherine, who had come to London and who by all accounts was reckoned to be drop-dead gorgeous. Whatever the reason, Montague had been very generous because all the Warden had to do was turn up to a few meetings and pocket the wages, which could be anything up to £2,000 a year. That's pretty good pay when you realize it is the equivalent of £1,000,000 a year these days!

Isaac wasn't the sort just to sit about and pocket the cash, and at the Mint he found a completely new sort of challenge waiting for him that he couldn't possibly resist. . .

British money was going through a crisis:

- About one in every five coins was a fake.
- Half of the real coins had been 'clipped', which means tiny bits of gold or silver had been snipped off. This would be melted down and sold.
- Foreign countries were starting to refuse to accept English coins.

If these problems weren't overcome quickly, then England would have gone bankrupt and the monarchy could have been overturned. This would have meant the return of the Catholics!

ISAAC'S UNDISCOVERED DIARY.

Not the Catholics! I hate their beliefs even more than the Church of England! And if Catholics take over, the land will be full of fighting again. And all my friends in good positions will be replaced by ignorant heretics! This can't happen! I must get straight to work!

The Mint was based in the Tower of London, and when Isaac first got there he found that his boss, Thomas Neale (the Master of the Mint), was lazy and useless. Before Neale had realized it, Isaac had moved into rooms right next door and taken over the running of the whole place.

To try and solve the money problem, the Mint had already started making a completely new set of coins which were harder to fake. They had much better prints on the heads and tails, and most importantly they had 'milled' edges. This means they had tiny little grooves round the sides (just like a 10p coin has today) which makes it obvious if a bit has been clipped off. These new coins weren't arriving nearly fast enough though, so Isaac's first job was to speed it up.

The Stuart Sun

August 1696

ALL CHANGE AT THE MINT!

The Warden of the Mint has installed new machines made to his design to produce coins eight times faster than before. 300 men and 50 horses are employed from 4 a.m. right through until midnight, producing well over £100,000 of new money each week.

An exhausted worker says, 'I just work one ten-hour shift, and that's enough! Sir Isaac sometimes works right through the whole 20 hours!'

Sir Isaac (53) was not available for comment. Apparently he was at work.

The new money flowing into the system made life harder for the 'clippers', but it did not solve the problem of all the fake coins that were appearing. Even though forgers could be punished by hanging, there were lots of people so poor that the temptation to make a few dud shillings was too much to resist – or it was until Isaac came along.

Isaac felt that the Mint's efforts were being regarded as a bit of a joke by the forgers, and he couldn't bear the idea of being laughed at. He wanted to shove the smiles right back into their smug faces, so he decided to go out and bring the forgers in himself.

This would have been a dangerous job for anybody, but especially so for Isaac. The only time he had really experienced anything like a pub before was 30 years previously when he had spent a short while living it up with Wickins. Now he found he had to visit all the nastiest, seediest and dirtiest dives in London to dig out his culprits.

At first Isaac wasn't too keen to enter this strange and sordid world, but like everything else he turned his mind to, he started to get rather good at it. Accompanied by some well-armed heavies he went in anywhere and everywhere to interrogate anyone he thought might have something to say. It wasn't so much Isaac's mean-looking assistants that scared people, but rather Isaac himself with his haggard face, silver hair, hawk eyes and awesome rage that would reduce the toughest nuts to mumbling jellies. Isaac also collected information from all over the country and there was even a special law to help him.

• Anybody who informed on a clipper got a reward.
• If an arrested clipper informed on two other clippers, he got let off.

Not surprisingly, people started talking. Isaac made a point of being at forgers' trials whenever he could and as a result hundreds were thrown in jail and dozens of them were hung with Isaac even signing their death warrants. Criminal society just didn't know what had hit it.

Isaac takes on Mr Big

Nearly all the forgers and clippers were from the backstreets, but there was one major player who lived rather grandly in Kensington. William Chaloner rather fancied himself, but although he lived in high society, hardly anyone knew how he made his money. He claimed to be an inventor, and he even had the nerve to suggest the Mint's machines should be replaced with his own. Of course Isaac, secretive as ever, utterly refused to

175

let Chaloner anywhere near the place and so Chaloner thought he'd stir things up a bit. He accused Isaac's machines of making forgeries.

ISAAC'S UNDISCOVERED DIARIES

Accused of forgeries!!! Never! Everything I do is pure, researched, refined beyond criticism. But suppose Chaloner is believed? Suppose my work is made open to inspection! They might find my secret thoughts about religion, they may learn of my private practices in the pursuit of alchemy! This could all be damning to me if discovered! I must silence Chaloner. I must **I MUST**

If Chaloner had thought his allegation was supposed to be funny, he had made a big, big mistake. Isaac set up an investigation on Chaloner, picking up every tiny whisper he could and he soon realized that Chaloner himself was a big-league counterfeiter. Isaac immediately had Chaloner pulled in, but Chaloner had friends in high places and he convinced them to help him get off. To Isaac's horror, Chaloner walked free.

Chaloner wasn't smug for long though, because when Isaac started something, he got it finished. Despite receiving death threats, he went all out to finish Chaloner off using bribery, intimidation and anything else it took to get the facts he needed. Chaloner managed to evade the law for 18 months, in which time he betrayed others to the gallows and even killed one or two informants himself – but it was never going to do him any good. When Isaac finally presented the case against him, it was absolutely concrete. If any of Chaloner's friends had tried to save him, it would have been like grabbing at fog. In a last attempt to save himself, Chaloner wrote a letter to Isaac pleading for his life.

In 1699 Chaloner was hanged, drawn and quartered at Tyburn, which was a popular place for such events. It's a bit hard to imagine somebody being hanged until nearly dead, chopped down, having their guts ripped out and burnt in front of their face, then being sawn into four quivering bits just outside Marks and Spencers at Marble Arch, isn't it? Still, that's where Tyburn was and that's what happened and everybody turned up with picnics to watch. Good clean family entertainment, wouldn't you say?

ISAAC'S SPARE TIME

For any normal person, working at the Mint and chasing forgers would have been far more than enough to be going on with. Of course for Isaac, every day had 24 hours, and very few of them were to be wasted on sleep.

One little diversion from sorting out the country's coins came from the German mathematician Leibniz, who had thought of a problem concerning gravity. Both he and his Swiss mathematical mate Bernoulli were completely stuck on it, so they challenged anybody else to come up with an answer.

When a copy of it reached Isaac after a long stint at the Mint, he declared that he refused to be teased by such silly puzzles. This was typical of him – remember at the time he was still keeping all his maths secret, and he was also having furious rows with Leibniz about calculus. However, the temptation was too much for Isaac and by the time he started work at 4 a.m. next morning, he had written out the solution. He sent it off without signing it, but Leibniz knew immediately where it had come from.

Although it was pretty cool to upset Leibniz by solving his little problem, Isaac also started upsetting someone who didn't deserve it.

John Flamsteed was the Astronomer Royal who we came across before, and you might remember he prided himself on plotting the movements of stars and planets as accurately as possible. His observations had been especially useful to Isaac while he was working on the *Principia*, so you might think that Isaac would have been grateful. Sadly, Isaac found it hard to acknowledge help from anyone else, and Flamsteed hadn't been impressed at the feeble mention he ended up with in the finished book, although he hadn't said much about it at the time. His feelings were made even worse because ages ago he had fallen out with Isaac's supporter Halley.

In 1694 Isaac was planning an updated version of the *Principia* and he started badgering Flamsteed for more detailed information about the moon. Flamsteed kindly agreed to supply it, but he needed to take his time to make sure all the observations and calculations involved were absolutely right. Over the months, Isaac got more and more impatient and when Flamsteed tried to hurry up, a few small mistakes started appearing.

179

Isaac got very cross about this, and suggested that Flamsteed should just stick to looking up his telescope and writing down what he saw. Flamsteed should give up trying to do even the simplest calculations because he wasn't good enough. This was extremely rude to a person of Flamsteed's abilities, and it didn't help that nobody dared to tell Isaac that he was being totally obnoxious. Poor old Flamsteed. For all his hard work and efforts, in the end all he got was abuse.

President Isaac

In 1699 Isaac was given Neale's job of Master of the Mint which he kept for the rest of his life. It brought him a massive pay rise which was fair enough as he had been the first Mint official in hundreds of years who had actually earnt it. However, the fun and games gradually started to die down and after a few years Isaac found he had more time on his hands.

In 1701 he resigned from being the Lucasian Professor and instead had another year as an MP. During this time he started releasing papers describing some of his early scientific work that he had kept so secret, but all the time he was really waiting for a new challenge.

It's at this point that we say goodbye to one of our leading characters in the book:

GLURK!

Yes, Robert Hooke died in 1703, but right up to the end he had kept his position as Secretary of the Royal Society.

AT LAST HE'S FINALLY HAD THE DECENCY TO DIE. NOW I ACCEPT!

Hang on Isaac, what are you accepting?

THE PRESIDENCY OF COURSE!

ROYAL SOCIETY

The Society took him on because obviously there was nobody to touch him for genius. There was also nobody to touch him for sheer bad manners either, because the very first thing he did was pull down Hooke's portrait from the wall and have it burnt.

The Society had got rather lazy over the previous years, and in particular the presidents had hardly bothered turning up. This wasn't Isaac's style at all, and he decided to make the whole thing more exciting again.

- He remembered the reactions he had had 30 years before when he had shown off his prisms and telescope, and so he arranged that every meeting should have a practical experiment for members to see.
- With Hooke out of the way, he was persuaded to release all his findings on light in his great book *Opticks*. He published it both in Latin and in English and made it as simple as possible, so that everybody could join in the fun.

• Along with *Opticks*, he also published his *Fluxions*. As we found out back on page 66, this led to a titanic clash with Leibniz who had published his calculus 20 years before. The two mental heavyweights made each other ill with accusations and abuse, and even after Leibniz died in 1716, Isaac never missed a chance to write or say something vile about him.

What with arguments, publications, demonstrations, burning portraits and everything, the society became a happening place again. Isaac must have been one of the main attractions himself as the broody but brilliant president, and in 20 years he only missed three meetings.

Sir Isaac

Yes indeed, in 1702 Isaac's friend William III fell to earth, then left it to join his late wife Mary. The throne went to Mary's sister, Anne, but the new queen had a difficult time trying to get everybody to support her. She started handing out honours to influential people and obviously Isaac as President of the Royal Society, Master of the Mint and greatest scientist ever known was high on her list. In May 1705 he was knighted.

A mean trick

Just because Isaac was having tantrums at Leibniz, this didn't mean he hadn't time to upset anybody else. As we know, he had already upset the Astronomer Royal, John Flamsteed, and things were to get worse. The Royal Observatory was run by the Royal Society, so as president it meant that Isaac was technically in overall charge of it.

Although Flamsteed did a lot of work for others – especially Isaac – his own work was the most important thing to him. For many years he had been charting the skies with his own equipment and keeping meticulous records for his own use, but suddenly Isaac decided he wanted the lot. He ordered Flamsteed to make everything available, but Flamsteed refused for as long as he could. This was awkward for him because other members of the Society saw Flamsteed as deliberately holding up the great work of the president.

Finally Isaac pulled a really mean trick. Queen Anne's husband George was no great genius, but he had declared a vague interest in astronomy. Isaac got him to commission a complete star guide, and obviously being the Astronomer Royal, Flamsteed could hardly refuse.

Poor Flamsteed was being asked to hand over his life's work for a pathetic sum of money, so he did everything he could to delay it. He managed to frustrate Isaac for seven years, but to his horror his old enemy Halley was finally given the job of editing and publishing everything he'd done. Four hundred copies were printed which made all Flamsteed's private studies available to anybody who could be bothered to look at it.

To add to his misery, when Isaac published the updated version of the *Principia*, he had removed almost every reference to Flamsteed despite using a lot of his data. It just shows what a really nasty person Isaac could be – even though he had always kept his own work as secret as possible, he couldn't care less about splattering Flamsteed's great efforts all over the place with hardly any payment and even less thanks. How mean can you get?

At least Flamsteed did manage a sad little gesture of revenge. A few years later he was given the chance to buy up most of the copies of his own book and he piled them up in the grounds of the Royal Observatory.

185

Isaac's baffling books

Even in his seventies, Isaac was still keeping himself busy with both the Royal Society and the Mint (and he was still sending forgers to the gallows). Leibniz tried to catch him out again with another fiendish puzzle, but as before, Isaac sat up all night to solve it, then went in to work as normal. Isaac also tried redrafting some of his religious beliefs to see if he could present them in an acceptable way, but it didn't work. (A few weeks before he died he made a point of burning a lot of papers which he claimed were just boring files from the Mint – but does that sound likely? It was probably something far more suspicious that nobody ever got to know about.) All in all, life cruised on rather unspectacularly apart from a couple of rather confusing books he wrote.

Chronology of the Ancient Kingdoms Amended

This rather fancy book title says that Isaac had managed to pin down the dates of events in distant history. The whole idea was rather clever: it was based on his studies of the night sky which had shown that over the centuries the patterns of stars and planets changed in a regular fashion. As many of the ancient texts he had read gave full details of the sky, Isaac realized that a reasonably good estimation of the dates of some of these old stories could be made. (For example, he calculated that the epic Greek tale of 'Jason and the Argonauts' occurred in 937 BC, which was a lot more recent than people had thought.) He was especially keen on stories about people like Moses in the Old Testament of the Bible, and he insisted that the ancient kingdom of Israel had been the first proper civilization, and that other civilizations like the Greeks and Romans had just followed on, developing their ideas.

Unfortunately this chronology book was such a crazy mixture of astronomy, scripture and maths that hardly anybody understood it. His very last book wasn't any better:

Observations on the Prophecies of Daniel and the Apocalypse of St John

Not only was the title equally un-catchy, it was a very dreary read based on the Bible studies he had been making for 50 years. The most interesting thing in it is that Isaac reckoned the world would end in the year 2132, so put it in your diary.

Both of these books were so odd that neither of them were published until after Isaac had died.

GRUMBLE
GRUMBLE
GRUMBLE

ISAAC GETS HIS FINAL ANSWER

Isaac was lucky in that, unlike most other people at the time, his health stayed with him right into his eighties. When he did start to get frail, it happened quickly, and he was looked after by his niece Catherine and her husband John Conduitt. In fact it was Conduitt who later decided to investigate and write as much about Isaac as he could, and it's thanks to him that we know as much as we do.

Isaac kept his spirits up to the end, and one nice little story is about him staggering along to a church. When he was offered a lift he grinned: 'Have legs, use legs.'

All too soon it was early morning, 20 March 1727.

HE'S GONE

GONE WHERE?

It was an interesting question, and one that Isaac had spent a lifetime wondering about. Just before he died a priest had come to see him, but Isaac had refused a final blessing. It was too late for his beliefs to upset anybody else or get him into trouble now. For Isaac, dying must have been the ultimate experiment in which he would get the final answer to the biggest question of all:

'Where is God?'

AFTER ISAAC

Isaac's body was buried in a grand ceremony in Westminster Abbey on 4 April 1727, but his work will survive for ever.

So did he get everything right?

The answer is YES.

Well, maybe not quite everything, but when you think that Isaac completely changed the whole way that we understand science, any little corrections we try to make seem rather pathetic. In fact, after 300 years, we've only found a few details that can be improved. One of these is that Isaac suggested a beam of light was made up of lots of very tiny particles.

I SUGGESTED IT WAS SOME SORT OF WAVE MOTION

Yes, but that's all it was, a suggestion. Neither of you were really sure, so get back in your coffin.

These days we know that light is a form of electomagnetic radiation which is the same sort of thing as radio waves. Does this mean that just for once Hooke came closer than Isaac? It seemed so for a long time, but recently scientists are starting to think that this radiation may involve strange particles after all. We could go into this, but after a whole book on Isaac, it's a bit late to hold our noses and dive into what's called 'quantum theory', so we'll leave it.

The other thing that Isaac didn't quite get right was $F = MA$ but it took 200 years for another genius to come along and tell us why. Albert Einstein had got concerned about what happened when things travelled at the speed of light, and eventually realized the equation needed a little tweak. Instead of $F = MA$, Albert said the equation should be:

$$F = \frac{MA}{\left(1 - \dfrac{v^2}{c^2}\right)^{\frac{3}{2}}}$$

(obviously v is your speed and c is the speed of light)

. . .but unless you are travelling at several thousands of kilometres per second, Albert's alteration won't make any difference.

FASTER! FASTER! I'LL PROVE NEWTON WRONG IF IT TAKES *FOREVER!*

ALICE BOWS OUT

One hundred and fifty-five summers had passed in the garden at Woolsthorpe since Alice had dropped her apple. Beneath her branches many generations of children had played and grown up and gone on to produce children of their own.

Alice may have wondered whether any of her own seeds had found a suitable place in which to set root and flourish. She could only be sure that if hers had not succeeded, then others had and so the natural cycle would continue. In recent years Alice's bark had started to harden, and a disease brought by the damp had managed to infest her inner body. Alice knew it was time to take her leave, and so it was one autumn morning that she became dimly aware of the regular hack of an axe at her base. She felt no pain and no regret after all, she had done everything that had been expected of her.

And so much more.